Twayne's English Authors Series

Sylvia E. Bowman, *Editor*

INDIANA UNIVERSITY

Algernon C. Swinburne

Algernon C. Swinburne

By JOHN A. CASSIDY

Indiana University

Twayne Publishers, Inc.   ::   New York

To
Margaret and John

Preface

As is the case with most major Victorian literary figures, Algernon Charles Swinburne has had to wait until the middle years of the twentieth century for anything like adequate treatment of his life and work. To materials concerning him, more than to almost any other prominent figure of his time, Victorian taboos were applied with such rigidity that only with the publication of Professor Cecil Y. Lang's six volumes of *The Swinburne Letters* (1959-1962) have many hitherto suppressed documents been released to the world.

We now know much about Swinburne that we did not know before or could only guess at. And because of such studies as Oswald Doughty's *Dante Gabriel Rossetti* (1949), Helen Rossetti Angeli's *Dante Gabriel Rossetti* (1949) and *Pre-Raphaelite Twilight* (1954), Margaret Gilman's *Baudelaire the Critic* (1943), and James Pope-Hennessy's *Monckton Milnes* (1951), we are able more accurately to gauge the effect of others upon him and to recreate the artistic and philosophical climate in which he lived and wrote. Always, of course, we doff the hat to the great French scholar Georges Lafourcade, whose *La Jeunesse de Swinburne* (1928) and *Swinburne* (1932), dynamited the ice jam of reticence and started the flow of new information.

The purpose of this book is to throw as much light upon Swinburne's literary works as possible. Biography enters the picture only where it is indispensable to a full understanding of the writings. But because Swinburne's works mirror his life very closely and because his brilliant mind ranged far, wide, and deep for its fare, I have had to deal extensively with such matters as Pre-Raphaelitism, Positivism, and French aestheticism. To account for and explain the unmistakable traces of sadism and masochism in his works, I have utilized some of the most recent research of modern psychiatry in the area of abnormal sexuality.

My scholarly debts are many and my gratitude great to those who have assisted materially in the preparation of this book: Theodore A. Hill, M.D., psychiatrist, and Grace Harris Hill, psychologist, gave generously of their time and professional knowledge. Professor Stanley Pargellis and the staff of the Newberry Library, Chicago, provided library facilities and assistance which were indispensable. Professor Thomas Souter and Mrs. Mary Baker of the Indiana University Library, Miss Mary Zimmermann and Mrs. Veronica Szasz of the South Bend-Mishawaka Campus Library were helpful in providing materials through interlibrary loan. Assistant Dean Jack J. Detzler of the South Bend-Mishawaka Campus relieved me of other duties, thus making it possible for me to give more time to research and writing.

The Summer Research Grant from the Graduate Research Division of the Indiana University Graduate School, John W. Ashton, Dean and Vice-President, gave me time and opportunity to collect many of the materials used in this study.

JOHN A. CASSIDY

Indiana University
April, 1964

Acknowledgments

I am grateful to Messrs. William Heinemann Ltd. for permission to quote from the Bonchurch Edition of Swinburne's *Complete Works* and for permission to obtain and use microfilmed copies from the British Museum of the still unpublished juvenilia.

Acknowledgment is also made to the following publishers for permission to print copyright material:

To the Yale University Press for selections from *The Swinburne Letters*, edited by Cecil Y. Lang.

To the Oxford University Press for selections from Georges Lafourcade's *La Jeunesse de Swinburne*.

To the Modern Language Association for permission to use in a different form material from my article, "Robert Buchanan and the Fleshly Controversy," *PMLA*, March, 1952.

Contents

Contents

Chronology

1837   Algernon Charles Swinburne born April 5 in Grosvenor Place, London, first of six children of naval captain Charles Henry Swinburne, the second son of Sir John Edward Swinburne, and Lady Jane Henrietta Hamilton Swinburne, the fourth daughter of the third Earl of Ashburnham.

1849   Algernon taken to Eton by his parents and placed in care of James Leigh Joynes, tutor.

1853   Leaves Eton in August and, for no announced reason, does not return, though normally he should have stayed two more years.

1854   Permission to enlist in cavalry is refused by father. Tutored for Oxford.

1856   January, journeys to Oxford with father; entered Balliol College with Benjamin Jowett as tutor. One of the original members of Old Mortality, an undergraduate literary and discussion society under the leadership of John Nichol.

1857   Writes poems and essays for *Undergraduate Papers,* a publication taken over by Old Mortality. November—he meets Dante Gabriel Rossetti, Edward Burne-Jones, and William Morris, who are painting murals in Oxford Union; Swinburne is fascinated with them and Pre-Raphaelitism; he begins to write poems and plays in Pre-Raphaelite style.

1859   Learns doctrine of "art for art's sake" from Pre-Raphaelites, takes trips to London to visit Rossetti and others. The attention given to writing verse leads to poor academic record.

1860   Leaves Oxford under questionable circumstances without degree. Publishes *Queen Mother* and *Rosamond.*

1861   Goes to Mentone with family; goes alone on journey to Italy. Father grants him annual pension of £200 and permission to live in London. Visits Richard Monckton Milnes (later Lord Houghton) at Fryston; meets Richard Burton at Fryston; after meeting Burton he begins to drink more.

1862   Reviews Victor Hugo's *Les Miserables* and Baudelaire's *Les Fleurs du Mal* in *Spectator*. Review of *Les Fleurs* is first statement of "art for art's sake" in Engand. Begins long friendship with Hugo. Introduced to works of Marquis de Sade by Milnes. Moves into Tudor House in Cheyne Walk with Dante Rossetti. Defends Meredith's *Modern Love* in letter to *Spectator*. Quarrels with Richard Holt Hutton and ends connection with *Spectator*.

1863   Visit to Paris with Whistler. Association with Simeon Solomon. Death of Edith Swinburne. Swinburne goes to visit his cousin Mary Gordon; he falls in love with her; works on *Atalanta in Calydon*.

1864   Suffers disappointment in love affair with Mary Gordon. Leaves Tudor House; coolness toward Dante Rossetti. Elected to Arts Club. Visits Walter Savage Landor in Florence.

1865   Publishes *Atalanta* with dedication to Landor. Family moves from "East Dene" to "Holmwood." *Atalanta* achieves real success. Friendship with George Powell. Publishes *Chastelard;* it encounters adverse criticism. Angers Lord Houghton and Tennyson at Moxon's dinner.

1866   Praises Baudelaire at annual dinner of Royal Literary Fund. Publication of *Poems and Ballads* raises storm in critical press. Breaks with Moxon's and agrees to publish with John Camden Hotten. Publishes *Notes on Poems and Reviews* in defense of *Poems and Ballads*.

1867   Meets Mazzini in March; is persuaded by him to write poems for Italian freedom. Begins notorious affair with Adah Isaacs Menken.

1868   Publishes critical volume *William Blake;* poem "Ave Atque Vale" in memory of Baudelaire; ends his interest in "art for art's sake." Nearly drowned at Étretat.

1870   Assists Dante Rossetti in preparing *Poems* for publication.

Has trouble with Hotten over publication of *Songs Before Sunrise.*

1871 Publishes *Songs before Sunrise.* To "Holmwood" to recuperate from dissipation. Renews excesses in July and becomes so ill his father closes his apartment and takes him home. In October Robert Buchanan publishes anonymous article "The Fleshly School of Poetry," attacking Rossetti and Swinburne.

1872 Publishes *Under the Microscope.* Termination of friendship with Dante Rossetti.

1873 Hotten's death frees Swinburne.

1874 Concludes publishing agreement with Andrew Chatto and publishes *Bothwell.*

1875 Publishes *Essays and Studies* and *George Chapman.* Considerable association with Jowett.

1876 Letter to *Athenaeum* attacking Furnivall. In court because of Buchanan's suit over Swinburne's publication of "Epitaph on a Slanderer" and "The Devil's Due" in *Examiner.* Verdict in Buchanan's favor. Publishes *Note on the Muscovite Crusade* attacking Carlyle.

1877 Father dies in March; back in London by June with money from inheritance; unrestrained dissipation.

1879 Health considerably and steadily worsened by excesses; Swinburne in very poor health when, early in June, Theodore Watts takes him from his rooms to house in Putney. Publishes *A Study of Shakespeare* in December.

1880 Quiet life at "The Pines" with Watts. Publishes *Songs of the Springtides* and *Studies in Song.*

1881 Continues quarrel with Furnivall; publishes *Euthanatos* and *Mary Stuart.*

1882 Death of Dante Rossetti. Journey to Paris in November for five days with Watts; first and last meeting with Hugo. Handicapped by deafness.

1883 Publishes *A Century of Roundels.*

1884 Publishes *A Midsummer Holiday and Other Poems.*

1885 Publishes drama *Marino Faliero.* Exchanges poem "A Word for the Navy" for some of his old letters to Howell. Death of Lord Houghton.

1886 Publishes *Miscellanies* and *A Study of Victor Hugo.* First meeting with T. J. Wise. Quarrel with John Churton Collins.

1887 *Publishes* poem "The Question," attacking Gladstone and Parnell; also publishes "The Jubilee," *Locrine,* and *Whitmania.*

1888 Attacks Whistler and repudiates "art for art's sake" in article "Mr. Whistler's Lecture on Art." Attacks Gladstone in "The Armada."

1889 Publishes *Poems and Ballads, Third Series.* Attacks Parnell and the Irish in "The Ballad of Truthful Charles."

1890 Death of Sir Richard Burton and William Bell Scott.

1891 Writes "Eton: An Ode for the Four Hundred and Fiftieth Anniversary," but refuses invitation to attend ceremony. Publishes memorial verses on Burton and Scott and a birthday poem to Tennyson.

1892 Intense anger at Scott when *Autobiographical Notes* published; publishes "The New Terror" in reprisal. Publishes *The Sisters, a Tragedy.*

1894 Publishes *Astrophel and Other Poems* and *Studies in Prose and Poetry.*

1896 Publishes *The Tale of Balen.* Saddened by death of his mother and William Morris.

1899 Publishes "A Channel Passage" and *Rosamund, Queen of the Lombards,* dedicated to Mrs. Disney Leith.

1903 Seriously ill with pneumonia.

1904 Publishes *A Channel Passage and Other Poems.*

1905 Marriage of Watts (now calling himself "Watts-Dunton") to Miss Reich, Watts's secretary. Swinburne publishes *Love's Cross-Currents.*

1908 Publishes *The Age of Shakespeare* and *The Duke of Gandia.*

1909 April 10, death from pneumonia.

CHAPTER 1

The Paths of Orthodoxy

IN 1836, one year after his promotion to a captaincy in the British Navy, Charles Henry Swinburne married his second cousin, Lady Jane Henrietta Hamilton. Both came from old aristocratic families. Charles Henry was a younger son of Sir John Swinburne of "Capheaton Hall," Northumberland; Lady Jane was the fourth daughter and one of twelve children of the third Earl of Ashburnham, of "Ashburnham Place," Sussex.

Both families were in good circumstances and surrounded with rich traditions stemming from English history. Both had been warm adherents of the Stuarts. The Ashburnhams, however, forsook the cause long before the Swinburnes, who remained Catholic and followed the deposed James II to France, where some of them continued to live and be educated until the time of Sir John Swinburne, the poet's grandfather. When Sir John inherited the title, he renounced Jacobitism, anglicized both his religion and his politics, and won the practical reward of a seat in Parliament in 1788.[1]

Although some three hundred miles separate Northumberland and Sussex, intermarriage between the two families was quite common and had been so long before the union of Captain Charles Henry and Lady Jane. They, for instance, were second cousins by virtue of their maternal grandfathers having been cousins. Moreover the Captain's cousin, Sir Henry Gordon, was married to Lady Jane's younger sister.

I *Hadji*

On April 5, 1837, about eleven weeks before eighteen-year-old Victoria fell heir to the British throne, Algernon Charles Swinburne was born in Grosvenor Place, London. Shortly afterward, Captain Swinburne moved his family to the Isle of Wight, where he rented "East Dene," a luxurious home with at least ten acres of lawn rolling down to the seashore. On the east coast of Wight, near the village of Bonchurch, the site had distinct advantages. It was only about sixty-five miles from London, an equal distance from "Ashburnham Place" in Sussex, and just across Spithead Channel from the great naval base at Portsmouth.

Here Swinburne grew up with his four sisters and brother. A few miles further inland on Wight was the home of Captain Swinburne's cousin, Sir Henry Gordon, and his wife Lady Mary, Lady Jane's younger sister. Their only child, Mary Gordon, some three years younger than "Cousin Hadji," as they called Algernon, often joined the Swinburne brood as they played about the beaches and roamed the lawns around "East Dene."

It was an ideal place for a happy childhood; the only drawback was that the Captain was often away on naval duty, with only occasional leaves at home. This left Lady Jane to manage the home and rear the young. Hadji was, therefore, rather hopelessly outnumbered, living in a matriarchy and surrounded by four sisters and a female cousin. Edward, the youngest child, was not born until a few months before his older brother had left for Eton in 1849.

Lady Jane devoted herself to her children. Much of her time was taken up with their education. Earnestly religious, she guided the feet of her charges toward High Church Anglicanism. In the little school she set up and presided over at "East Dene," the Bible was read regularly. When Hadji's reading ability had progressed to the point where he could do so, he was often called upon to read portions of the Scriptures aloud, a task which delighted him.[2] With the personal involvement of his ancestors in England's past, Lady Jane found it easy to engage her son's interest in history. The novels of Scott were then at the zenith of their popularity; and she, like many Victorian parents, directed Hadji's attention to them with marked success. Dickens, too, was rising rapidly; Hadji was so taken with *Dombey and Son* that he acted out scenes from it.[3] From Dickens and Scott, Lady Jane took her pupil to Shakespeare and Moliere. As a proper Victorian lady she made certain that it was the carefully expurgated *Family Shakespeare* of Thomas Bowdler, the "Victorianized" Shakespeare tailored to fit the rigid niceties of the proper Victorian home. Lady Jane had had Continental training which gave her a good command of French and Italian. These she labored to pass on to her son, along with the love of both countries that had much to do with his literary career.

The boy learned with astonishing rapidity. Not only was he quick to comprehend and assimilate, but he rarely forgot. His memory was the kind that fills ordinary people with despair. Poems, for instance, that he had heard only once or twice, he could repeat verbatim long afterward. Had the rest of him only equaled his mind, he would have gladdened the hearts of his parents! But nature, in one of her compensatory quirks, had given him disadvantages to detract from his brilliance. His appearance was grotesque. His huge head, covered with carroty red hair, was out of proportion to his slight body and dainty hands and feet. The head rested upon a short, thick neck. His narrow shoulders sloped so as to be almost nonexistent. In size he was diminutive, and his voice, always high pitched, often rose with excitement until it became a screech. To make matters worse, from early childhood he was afflicted with a nervousness which caused his arms and hands to twitch as though he had St. Vitus's dance. When he walked, he had a bobbing, springing motion which made him noticeable anywhere.

One can imagine that when he appeared at Ashburton Place or for the longer visits to "Capheaton Hall," where old Sir John loved to gather his twenty-four grandchildren about him in the summer, members of both families must have looked at one another in amazement and wondered how and why this dwarfed, malformed fruit had appeared on their virile family trees. One can imagine too that his effeminacy, his delicacy, his lack of vigor and coordination stood out most glaringly when he attempted to take part in games with other children.

Towards such a child, a mother tends to be more than ordinarily protective; the father, knowing the stern demands of a man's world, can hardly conceal his dismay. An age gap of forty years existed between Swinburne and his father; not an impassable barrier, but still an obstacle to a close relationship. Add to this that the father was much away from home and boy, and we have another barrier. The two had been formed in different worlds: the Captain had begun his naval training at the age of twelve and had twenty-seven years of stern naval discipline behind him when Algernon was born; the boy, as has been seen, grew and took form in a feminine environment, indulged, pampered, and perhaps even treated as another girl.

Such straws are not conclusive but may be indicative. Because of the scarcity of reliable information about Swinburne's childhood and family relationships, we have to use whatever scraps are available to fill in the gaps with conjectures. That the relationship between Swinburne and his father was not one of sympathy and understanding is clear from a letter he wrote to William Rossetti on January 15, 1870. Defending Shelley against Rossetti's charge of unfilial treatment of his father, Swinburne takes pains to explain what he regards as Shelley's justification:

. . . I think you are rather hard upon him as to the filial relation. . . . I have no doubt that it may be said for Sir Timothy that his son was what Carlyle calls "an afflictive phenomenon" than that I was the same to my father before, during, and since my Oxford time; but I do not think you make allowance for the provocation given (as well as received) by a father, who may be kindly and generous, to a boy or man between seventeen and twenty-one or so, with whom he has no deep or wide ground of sympathy beyond the animal relation or family tradition. You will allow me to say that I am sure you can never have felt at that age the irreparable, total and inevitable isolation from all that had once been closest to the mind and thought, and was still closest to the flesh and the memory, the solitude in which one passes from separation to antagonism of spirit (without violent quarrels or open offense, but by pure logical necessity of consequence) the sense that where attraction gradually ends repulsion gradually begins, which many besides Shelley, and as affectionate and faithful by nature and temperament as he, *have* felt at that age.[4]

Swinburne is speaking of Shelley, but who can doubt that he is defending himself as well? He does not say how long before his "Oxford time" he was an "afflictive phenomenon" to his father toward whom he had an "antagonism of spirit." Perhaps he was not aware. Such aversions do not spring up over night, but are a slow, gradual growth. Sometime during boyhood he became aware that he and his father had almost nothing in common; and when, even before he went to Eton, he began to write and, with his sisters and cousin, to act out extravagant dramas, his efforts met with little understanding from his father, whose hobbies ran to mechanics and woodworking rather than to the arts.

Towards his mother his feeling was altogether different. Upon her he concentrated the affection that should have gone to both parents. She was his protectress, his tutor, his intellectual guiding light—the one who always understood and to whom he could turn for sympathy. The strong bond between them never weakened. Even after he lost his religious faith, she never ceased to believe that he would return to the religion of his childhood and, at every opportunity, she urged him to do so. Throughout her life she was the strongest single influence upon him; her death in 1896 left a void never to be filled.

All this brings us to a consideration of the matter which is central to Swinburne's life, character, and literary work—the question of his abnormal tendencies. There is no direct, positive evidence that Swinburne was a homosexual. Several of his letters to his Bohemian friends contain implications of this nature—as do some guarded references to him in the letters of William Bell Scott, Lady Trevelyan, and his mother. Still, implications and guarded references are not final proof. But whether or not he was a homosexual is not of the first importance to an understanding of his works. What is of the greatest importance is that strong traces of abnormal tendencies show up very clearly in his works and often are the factors which determine their fundamental character.

This matter is considered early in this study for a good reason. Recent research into homosexuality by a group of psychiatrists using case histories of over one hundred homosexuals they had treated as patients shows that the detachment of the father from the son either by absence or lack of sympathy is a factor which tends to encourage homosexuality and to prevent recovery from it.[5] Swinburne's father was physically absent until his retirement in 1857, when Swinburne was twenty; and he was detached mentally and temperamentally in the other ways we have noted. By all reports and evidence he was a good father who labored to understand and to do the right thing for his difficult son. But in Swinburne's mind he was aloof and unsympathetic, as the letter to William Rossetti shows. The psychological effect was probably just as baneful as it would have been if Swinburne's father had been what the son thought he was.

The same study of homosexuality shows that another factor often present in cases of abnormality is an overly possessive and indulgent mother, especially one who creates or encourages the impression that she alone loves the son and the father does not.[6] Under the circumstances Lady Jane could have unwittingly given such an impression, and her defense of her ugly duckling could have helped it along. Swinburne, of course, could have formed the impression, whether it was warranted or not. True or imagined, the total effect would have been equally harmful.

Although Swinburne found little in his father that he could idealize, for old Sir John Swinburne, his father's father, he had a profound admiration. Every summer the Swinburnes would journey to "Capheaton Hall" to spend several weeks in its romantic neighborhood. Lying less than forty miles from the Cheviot Hills and the Scottish Border, the residence and the countryside were rich in border history and ballads. Even more interesting than the countryside was old Sir John himself, an inexhaustible source of legend and history and a link with the romantic past. Born in France in 1762, the old patriarch was seventy-five when Hadji arrived in the family in 1837. The old man and his redheaded grandson soon discovered that they had more in common with each other than with their intermediate link, Captain Charles Henry, who represented a more unimaginative, plodding strain in the family. Swinburne bestowed upon Sir John all the love and admiration he denied his own father; and, since the grandfather lived until 1860, they had twenty-three years of association.

Sir John was the man that Swinburne wanted vainly to be. A dashing, romantic figure, goodlooking enough in his youth to be a movie idol in the twentieth century, he was a rebel and a republican who had been friends with Mirabeau and Wilkes. Moreover, he had a sensitive appreciation for literature which revealed itself in the many French titles in the library at "Capheaton Hall," in his presidency of the Literary and Philosophical Society of nearby Newcastle-on-Tyne, in his activities in the Society of Antiquaries, and in his close association with Leigh Hunt. His love of painting led to a friendship with Mulready and to pictures by Mulready and Turner for the gallery at "Capheaton Hall." To Swinburne he was a link with the Old France of pre-Revolutionary days, as well as with the bloody times of the Revolution when Paris mobs stormed the Bastille and beheaded a king. More important, he was a direct contact with such glamorous figures as Byron and

Shelley. A cavalier of the old school, he loved to ride to the hunt; and on one occasion he had had a shooting accident which blew out a piece of his skull and necessitated trepanning.

In a biographical letter to E. C. Stedman in 1875, Swinburne's only mention of his father is that he is Sir John's second son; then for some five hundred words he tells lyrically of the virtues and exploits of Sir John. Admiringly he says: "It is said that the two maddest things in the North country were his horse and himself; but I don't think the horse can have been the madder. . . ." [7] Telling of the old man's death at ninety-nine, he adds fondly and wistfully: ". . . he was most kind and affectionate to me always as child, boy, and youth."

In Swinburne's life Sir John stood at the head of a procession of older men to whom he turned for affection and guidance. After the grandfather came John Nichol, Dante Gabriel Rossetti, Lord Houghton, Benjamin Jowett, Walter Savage Landor, Mazzini, William Rossetti, William Bell Scott, and Theodore Watts-Dunton. Of all these, perhaps the truest and kindest was Sir John.

II *The River and the Flogging-Block*

Had Swinburne been a normal boy, nothing would have been more natural than for Captain Swinburne to have groomed him for the Naval College and a career like his own. But Swinburne was not a normal boy, and such a career was as far beyond his reach as the moon. The question was what to do with him. His ability and delight in learning were remarkable, his religiosity was pronounced, his flow of words when speaking on a subject near his heart was astounding. These added up to a career in the Church. A career in the Church necessitated a university degree. Eton, Oxford, and then the Church was the course planned by the parents.

The Captain and Lady Jane looked ahead with dread to the impact of the harsh discipline of Eton upon their rebellious, in-dulged little scion. To get him ready, they chose the Reverend C. Foster Fenwick of nearby Brook Rectory as tutor. Whether Swinburne had to endure anything like the brutal floggings dealt Bertie Seyton by Denham in *Lesbia Brandon* is doubtful. To get him ready for the heavy arms of Eton tutors, the Captain might have instructed Fenwick to lay on a few light floggings when

Hadji was lazy or defiant; but Lady Jane would have hardly stood for anything more.

Their concern was all the greater because Hadji was showing those signs of extreme nervousness that stayed with him throughout his life: the excitability; the trembling and jerking of the hands, arms, and, when seated, feet and legs; the rising of the voice to a screech; the seemingly uncontrollable gush of words. What would be the outcome when such spells came on him at Eton? Shortly before he left, Lady Jane took him to a specialist who advised that the condition was the result of too much "electric vitality," which if any attempt were made to stop it could have bad effects.[8]

Consequently, when the time arrived for Hadji to go to Eton in April, 1849, Lady Jane went along with her husband and the boy, even though she had to leave nine-month-old Edward to do so. One can imagine that her purpose was to make certain that Tutor James Leigh Joynes, in whose care Algernon was to be entrusted, knew to the full what the specialist had said so as to extend every possible consideration to this special case. Further aid was sought from Swinburne's cousin, Algernon Bertram Mitford, who, though only five weeks older, had already been at Eton three years, and whom the anxious parents asked to aid Hadji in his adjustment to his new environment.

Perhaps, also, Lady Jane privately asked Mrs. Joynes, the sympathetic, motherly wife of Tutor Joynes, to keep an eye on Hadji and to report to her from time to time on how he was faring in the severe, masculine environment of Eton. She effected such liaison years afterward with his landladies in London; she would hardly have missed the opportunity to have made such an arrangement with Mrs. Joynes. At any rate, the tutor's wife stood out in Swinburne's memory in an emollient light; for, when his mother wrote him in 1882 that Mrs. Joynes had died, his reply paid a grateful tribute to her "who was so infinitely kind to me, at an age when I most needed kindness." [9]

As anyone who knows boys could have predicted, Swinburne's career at Eton was a stormy one. His cousin Algernon Mitford (later Lord Redesdale) and Sir George Young, the only two students who are mentioned as having been close to him, insist that the other boys let him alone because of a certain quality about him that boded trouble for anyone who attempted to bully him. But one wonders if they were not simply trying to shield his memory in the time-honored tradition of British biography and in accordance with the code of "the old school tie."

Other reports are much more in harmony with Swinburne's character as reported in his adult life, and indeed as he himself displays it in his letters—as one whose intellectual snobbery and vanity led him to trample on the feelings and rights of others to the point of insufferability. Sir Edmund Gosse, Swinburne's first biographer, tells of his dumping a pot of jam on the head of a maid because he did not like the way she read Shakespeare to him and of his standing up in bed and spouting poetry in a wild manner, frightening a well-meaning attendant who brought him a dose of medicine.[10] By 1853, his last year at Eton, he had earned the nickname "Mad Swinburne," [11] and the head boy of one of the halls pointed to him and advised a group of new entrants to kick him if they got close enough—and, if not near enough, to throw a stone at him.[12]

The trouble was, of course, that the system at Eton was based upon rigid discipline at every turn of the way—discipline in studies, in deportment, and among the students themselves. Failure to prepare lessons well usually resulted in a flogging; insolence or bad conduct could mean the same thing. The flogging-block was an institution at Eton, an accepted feature of the school; floggings were administered publicly; and, by several admissions in Swinburne's letters, he was officially present on several occasions. The practice of "fagging," by which a younger boy became a servant of an older boy and could be flogged by him for careless performance of such duties as running errands, waking him in the morning, and serving him at meals was another Eton tradition. We have no information as to whose fag Swinburne was, which in itself may be significant of an unhappy relationship with an older boy that his family and friends have labored to conceal; otherwise Swinburne or his cousin Algernon Mitford would have alluded to his fagging experience. We have no such allusion.

All his life Swinburne rebelled at discipline of any kind. It galled him and usually sent him in the opposite direction from the one intended. To attempt to adapt him to Eton discipline was like trying to fit a square peg into a round hole; by no means was the effort successful, and both the peg and the hole bore the scars of the attempt.

One good result of his unpleasant experiences with other boys was that it made him reclusive and turned him even more to books for companionship. In his studies, largely classical with some mathematics, Italian, and French, he did well, though not brilliantly. The core of the curriculum was what it had been from medieval days—Latin and Greek. The old standbys in these two languages were read, translated, and memorized—this last to the tune of two hundred to three hundred lines a week; in addition, the boys wrote imitative exercises in the same sacred Latin or Greek as the originals. They were permitted, even encouraged, to read Shakespeare—but only for the purpose of rendering him into Greek.

Out of this, Swinburne acquired a good foundation in classical lore and literature which left a strong imprint upon his later writings. He also developed a feeling for the structure of language and the roots of words, as well as for the infinite variety of nuances and accents underlying all composition, prose or verse. From the imitative exercises, some of which still repose in the British Museum with Joynes' commendations on them, he learned much of the mechanics of prosody.

His love of French led him to increase his knowledge of that language so greatly that he won the Prince Consort's Prize for Modern Languages in 1852, though he gave his mother's early training more credit than he did himself or Mr. Tarver, his teacher at Eton. Tarver also introduced him to such works of Victor Hugo as *Le Roi s'amuse, Notre-Dame de Paris,* and *Lucrece Borgia.* So delighted was Swinburne that Hugo remained an idol throughout his life and exerted a profound influence upon Swinburne's own work. When *Les Châtiments* appeared, Swinburne caught from it both a hatred of "Napoleon the Little" and a great admiration for Hugo's power of invective—which had much to do with his own delight in hurling the thunderbolts.

Most of these efforts were in the line of duty and in obedience to the system. But his truly remarkable intelligence enabled him to do the required work in a minimum of time; then he devoted himself to a wide exploration of English literature, using Eton's excellent libraries to do so. In his four and a half years at Eton he gave himself easily the equivalent of a present-day college major in English. He did this reading entirely on his own initiative, for none of it was required. The Elizabethan dramatists were his chief delight, and he covered them thoroughly. He did not, however, neglect Chaucer, Spenser, Milton, Pope, Prior, Thomson, Young, Wordsworth, Coleridge, Keats, Shelley, Moore, or Landor. In Landor he discovered a kindred rebel spirit; like Hugo, he also became a lifelong idol.

But he did more than read and assimilate. He tried his own wings in imitative flights of poetic fancy. Even before he came to Eton he had written several bloodcurdling dramas. Now he turned his hand to another, called *The Unhappy Revenge* in imitation of Tourneur's *The Revenger's Tragedy*. The revenge in Swinburne's play is the betrayal of ancient Rome to the Huns by the heroine Eudoxia as a reprisal for the wrong done her honor by the Emperor Maximus. An extravagant piece of fustian, it shows little promise of what was to come. Few boys of twelve or thirteen, however, would have stuck with it for four acts, as Swinburne did.

We have one other piece of juvenilia from Eton days, "The Triumph of Gloriana," in honor of the visit of Queen Victoria and Prince Consort Albert to Eton on June 4, 1851. Quick to capitalize upon the occasion for pedagogical purposes, some of the masters issued orders that the boys were to memorialize the event in heroic couplets as a substitute for the regular weekly composition in Latin. Swinburne displayed exceptional powers in catching the heavy beat and general tone of the Age of Reason.

> *What Muse shall boldly raise a humble lay,*
> *To celebrate the glories of this day?*
> *When glittering myriads flock, a countless crowd,*
> *Confus'd, with hearts upraised and voices loud;*
> *A thousand shouts the spacious triumph fill'd;*
> *No heart, no tongue was then by silence chill'd.*
> *What means this pomp: and what this festal throng,*
> *That down the crowded way is borne along?*
> *'Tis Gloriana now her palace seeks;*
> *And in that single voice wide Albion speaks.*[13]

For two hundred lines "The Triumph" with its heavy, regular beat rolls on like a parade of caissons. Eton, "the Temple of

Loyalty," is Athens; rival Harrow is lightly ridiculed as "the Theban mountain," obscured and dimly seen because "wrapt in a mist." The classical motif is carried out with Wellington as Miltiades.

Despite its faults we have here something more than a school exercise. Although fettered in heroic couplets, the poem has an undersurge of power and music out of the ordinary—almost as though it were straining to break through the shell of eighteenth-century formalism into the freedom and lyricism of *Atalanta in Calydon* or the "Song of Italy." A poet was emerging.

In the summer of 1853, two or three years before he normally would have, Swinburne left Eton, never to return. Because Eton has never spoken on the matter, we still do not know precisely why Swinburne left. Gosse intimates that the trouble centered about Swinburne's rebellion against Joynes' discipline and about his loss of interest in his studies.[14] Obviously Eton did not appreciate him or realize that in him she had a future great poet on her hands. Because he got his work so quickly and easily, he was known as an idler. The headmaster bluntly told Captain Swinburne that his son was "one of the idlest boys in the school," a charge which Swinburne denied almost forty years later as "a beastly lie" [15]

There was no love lost between him and Eton; he and she were not at all in harmony, though they did bear with each other for four and a half years. He was not expelled from Eton: he finished the term apparently in good order, went home, and that was the end. What, then, was the reason?

Apparently the answer lies in the fact that adolescence brought with it abnormal tendencies toward masochism and sadism which in 1852-53 became so noticeable that the Eton authorities had to reckon with them. In a boys' school like Eton, the faculty and administration would certainly have known about and have been on the alert to detect the mental and physical disturbances sometimes accompanying adolescence. Because of Swinburne's delicacy and effeminacy, they could hardly have been oblivious to the possibility of latent sexual abnormality becoming stronger and more evident during puberty. Such symptoms manifested themselves all too clearly in his growing delight in flagellation.

In later years he confided to Lord Houghton his joy at being whipped at Eton,[16] and he wrote another friend and former

Etonian that the only two things he could like to see at Eton were the Thames and the flogging-block.[17] The tenor of the letter leaves no doubt that the block interested him far more than the river. To Houghton also he recounted with evident relish that for one notable flogging given him by Joynes he was permitted to soak his face in eau de cologne to heighten the pleasure.[18] This indicates either that Joynes was also abnormal or that he was playing along with the boy to discover the full extent and meaning of his strange reactions. I think the latter, for Joynes was so well thought of at Eton that he was later offered the headmastership and refused it.

The nature of the case once discovered or strongly suspected, Joynes would have been duty bound to report it to the administration. From that time on, Swinburne would have been under the closest surveillance by all his masters. Since the punishment of the younger boys was administered in public at the flogging-block and since in many of his letters and other writings Swinburne tells of his joy in watching floggings, he could have no more stayed away from the block than a pyromaniac could stay away from a fire. His joy there would have been equally evident and significant to alert eyes. Once they became certain of his affliction, the authorities had to get him out of Eton for his sake and for the welfare of the other boys and the reputation of the school.

We do not know whether Joynes or Provost Hawley wrote Swinburne's parents of their suspicions and described the symptoms, or whether Joynes told Mrs. Joynes to write Lady Jane that her son's nervous condition had become so seriously aggravated that he should not return to Eton after the close of the current term. The latter is more likely. In either case, the situation was handled quietly and tactfully out of consideration for the boy, the parents, and the school.

How much Swinburne may have known of what was happening to him emotionally and of its effect upon others is unknown. He never forgave Eton. In 1891, when the headmaster asked him for an ode in honor of Eton's four hundred and fiftieth anniversary, Swinburne wrote a formal poetic tribute to the old school's role in training England's great men. Later he chuckled with glee in a letter to William Rossetti at how he had flung "the name of their *other* typical naughty boy and disgrace to the orthodox traditions of the school full in the face of the authorities, who I *trust* will be in a due and proper rage (not for the first time, I should suppose) with both of us." [19] Shelley's was the only name mentioned in the ode.

Swinburne also wrote a burlesque of the formal ode, calling it "Eton: Another Ode." Like the formal ode, it is in rhyming triplets and in anapestic-heptameter; it ruefully, playfully sings of some of his experiences at the block, probably—as the saying goes—with more truth than poetry.

> *"Tell me, S[winburn]e, does shame within burn as hot*
> *(Swish! Swish!) as your stripes my lad,*
> *Burn outside, have I tamed your pride? I'm glad to see how it*
> *hurts you—glad—*
> *Swish! I wish it may cure you. Swish! Get up." By Jove, what*
> *a dose I've had.*[20]

Can we doubt that Swinburne's real sentiments were in the burlesque rather than in his formal ode? In Swinburne's mind Eton was synonymous with flagellation, a subject ominously delightful to him until his death.

CHAPTER 2

Oxford and the Pre-Raphaelites

FOR two and a half years after leaving Eton, Swinburne led a leisurely existence at "East Dene," "Northcourt," and "Ashburnham Place." In 1854 his desire to enlist in the cavalry for service in the Crimean War was thwarted by his father's firm veto. In 1855 his uncle, General Thomas Ashburnham, took him on a five-week tour to Germany, which left Swinburne rather unimpressed. Throughout the two and a half years, he dutifully tutored for Oxford with neighboring clergymen both at "East Dene" and "Capheaton."

Much more enthusiastic was his pursuit of his ambition to be a poet. Here he found a sympathetic ally in Lady Trevelyan, wife of Sir Walter Trevelyan of "Wallington," an estate a short distance from "Capheaton." Childless and thirty-eight years old in 1854, Lady Trevelyan was free to pursue her interests in painting and literature. Ruskin and William Bell Scott, the Scottish painter-poet who later became one of Swinburne's close friends, were often at her home during the 1850's. In her, Swinburne found one of the few genuine friends of his life and the first perceptive, understanding believer in his poetic genius. She encouraged him to write verses and then to bring them to "Wallington" to read them to her.

The interim was soon over. Oxford and the adult world lay ahead, and Swinburne, at nineteen, turned toward it eagerly. In the four and a half years he was to encounter some of the strongest formative influences of his life; there, he would adopt many of the leading ideas and develop some of the characteristics that were to loom large in his later career.

During these same four and a half years, the Crimean War would drag itself to a close, in 1856, the savage and unnecessary Sepoy Rebellion would run its course, and the situation between the Southern and Northern American states would worsen until the Civil War became inevitable. Britain's dread of the growing power of the French Emperor Louis Napoleon would manifest itself in her sympathy for the assassination attempt of Felice Orsini, and the cause of Italian freedom would be greatly enhanced by the French defeat of Austria in 1859. All in all, it was an interlude in which the world's stage would be readied for the great actors and events of the 1860's and 1870's.

I The Student of Balliol

On January 23, 1856, Swinburne and his father journeyed to Oxford, where Swinburne was duly enrolled as a student in Balliol College with the already prominent Benjamin Jowett as his tutor. Captain Swinburne later remarked that Jowett was not the tutor he would have preferred for his son, possibly because he thought Jowett too mild and sympathetic for such a mettlesome charge as Algernon, but in the long run the boy could not have done better. Jowett was already Regius Professor of Greek and soon to become Master of Balliol; today his is one of the great names in the history of British scholarship and of brilliant teachers.

Because he did not early discover Swinburne's genius, some biographers have censured Jowett for lack of insight, but the pupil, too, must share the onus. Jowett's Classicism may have rendered him unsympathetic to such an unrestrained Romantic as Swinburne, but Swinburne was antagonistic to anyone in a pedagogical robe. Jowett, like most college professors, was ready and eager to be a friend to any student; but he expected the student to make the first overtures. Swinburne did not make them. Later, when Jowett discovered that his pupil was being led into dangerous paths by the Pre-Raphaelites, he did all he could to effect a rescue, but it was too late. The master must have held himself somewhat responsible for the loss of his sheep; for in 1868, when he heard that Swinburne was in a dire plight in London, he came forward with an offer of friendship Swinburne eagerly accepted. For the next twenty-five years, till Jowett's death in 1893, his was a stabilizing influence—one of the comparatively few good influences in Swinburne's life.

During his first year at Oxford Swinburne became friends with John Nichol, four years older than he. Nichol was a transfer to

Oxford after four years at the University of Glasgow, where his father was professor of astronomy and where he himself later rose to the rank of professor of English literature. When they met in 1856 Nichol was twenty-three and Swinburne nineteen, not a great disparity in terms of years, but a wide gulf in terms of maturity, especially if the older man has the additional advantages of education and worldly experience. Nichol had such advantages. When they first met, Swinburne was a freshman greeting a cynical and witty upperclassman who had traveled, had met Mazzini, had adopted such republican principles as a belief in Italian freedom and a hatred of Napoleon III, and had rejected religious orthodoxy as puerile nonsense.

Through his reading of Hugo and perhaps through the influence of Sir John Swinburne, Swinburne already disliked Napoleon III and was sympathetic to Mazzini and the cause of Italian freedom. He was not yet ready to deny Christianity, but he was questioning it. So complete was Nichol's domination that in short order Swinburne became a rabid foe of Napoleon III, a devoted proponent of Mazzini, and a scorner of Christianity generally and of Roman Catholicism in particular.

None of these attitudes was unusual for the time, and the only one that would have been frowned upon by the Oxford authorities was the rejection of religion. Even that would have been reprimanded mildly because religious opinions at Oxford were at that time in a state of upheaval. Since more than half of the students were in orders or planning to be, theological matters came in for considerable attention in and out of the classroom. The aftereffects of the Oxford Movement and of the defection of Newman to Roman Catholicism in the 1840's still hung in the air at the old university. The persistent stream of young Oxfordites who followed after Newman gave rise to a suspicion in the country at large that Oxford was a hotbed of Roman Catholic subversion, of which the professors were the traitorous gardeners.

Actually, of course, the religious roads ran out of Oxford in three directions. The high road still led to Anglicanism, though one side of it favored High Church and the other Low; a smaller bypath led to Roman Catholicism; a third road—growing in importance—belonged to those who repudiated the Bible, Christianity, and all formalized religion, adopting in their stead a vague agnosticism which accepted the idea of a great creative force or principle, but ridiculed as childish the concept of an anthropomorphic deity.

The last was the road taken by Nichol and toward it he directed the steps of Swinburne. Evidently a most important step in the "conversion" of the neophyte was to convince him that his faith had been imposed upon him by his parents when he was too young to know better. In an essay written during his Oxford days called "The Limits of Experience," Swinburne remarks with complete gravity and certainty: "That much which is with us a matter of real and universal acceptance—much which has come to be regarded as intuitive and as it were indispensable to our existence and faculty of thinking—is indeed mere matter of experience and previous acquaintance removed beyond the limit of consciousness or memory, is an evident truth." [1] Listing ideas of power, love, liberty, and religion as among the items which lie beyond memory, he states that such concepts are imparted to the infant in his very early childhood by his parents. Religion is put at the end of the list as though he hesitates to touch it, but then he follows doggedly his reasoning to its bitter conclusion. As he sees it, there is no absolute conviction because there is no absolute truth. All his beliefs and convictions have been inherited—in his case they had come from a mother whose education and intellectual attainments were far below his because she had never had the advantages of the university. Since they are that and nothing more, why should he not now abandon them? Under the aegis of Nichol, abandon them he did and for life. In his famous letter to Stedman in 1875, he admits he has been brought up a "quasi-Catholic," but he denies that he had ever accepted the idea of a personal God. Therefore the loss of his faith has left him only with "a turbid nihilism," transformed after a time into Positivism, the worship of "the divine humanity, the ideal of human perfection and aspiration, without worshipping any God, any person, any fetish at all." [2]

This view, of course, was precisely that held by Nichol and countless other Victorian intellectuals who, shying away from the term "atheist," disdained any form of religious belief. Swinburne's reaction was more than disdainful; for the rest of his life he was an implacable foe of Christianity and seldom missed an opportunity to sneer at it in his writings.

At first glance this is surprising. Because his religion had come principally from his mother, toward whom his devotion never lessened, we would expect him to regard his lost faith with the gentle sadness that characterizes Matthew Arnold's religious poetry. Arnold, however, influenced by his father's developmental theory of history, regarded Christianity and other forms of religion as necessary and useful stages in the evolution of man's thought, much as he might have looked upon the Roman chariot in the evolution of transportation. But to Swinburne, all religions, and Christianity especially, were but gigantic hoaxes promulgated by tyrants like Napoleon III and the Pope to enslave the masses politically through religious superstition. Accordingly, he hated both the exploiters and their tools, the clergy. Instead of blaming his mother, he saw her as an innocent victim.

Another factor conducing to the loss of his faith was his growing awareness of his sexual abnormality. He knew he was not like other young men his age; if he did not know why, their sneers and jeers would soon have told him. His failure to develop normally must have been of such concern to both him and his parents that they must have sought the advice of a specialist like the one Lady Jane took him to before he went to Eton. One can imagine that, after talking with the worried parents, the good man took Algernon aside and told him that because of unknown factors of heredity he would never have the manly muscles, voice, appearance, or desires of other young men; that this was an affliction put upon him by God's will and one that he must bear prayerfully and patiently as a personal cross. One can imagine Algernon's initial shock turning into passionate complaint and then into savage denunciation of God for causing this affliction. When Nichol and atheism came along, he welcomed them. It was a senseless, nihilistic universe; his own calamity proved the point.

As a man thinks, so he is and so he writes. Nihilism is the poorest kind of basis for the artist. It is fatal to idealism, to optimism, to compassion, to hope. The long-range effect upon Swinburne's writings was to make them negative, pessimistic, and denunciatory. His muse was fated to fly with crippled wings. Where she might otherwise have soared over the mountain peaks, she did well to clear the tree tops.

Nichol's influence was increased when, in November, 1856, he gathered Swinburne and four other Oxonians in his rooms to form a literary-discussion group under the name "Old Mortality," a title based on the claim that all six members had at one time or another been close to death from ill health and were still frail. They soon won a campus reputation as revolutionaries. As organizer and presiding genius, Nichol set the tone. They met weekly in one another's rooms; read essays and poems, some original; and discussed literary matters. Their readings and discussions show clearly their unorthodox character. Nichol read an essay on Wycliffe; Swinburne read Browning's "The Statue and the Bust," with its unorthodox approval of adulterous love; his "The Heretic's Tragedy" and "Bishop Bloughram's Apology," both heavily satirical of religious hypocrisy; and Morris's "The Defence of Guinevere," which, like "The Statue and the Bust," flaunted Victorian standards of morality.

To read and discuss are well enough; but how much more satisfying it is to see one's views in print. Accordingly, the society established a magazine in November, 1857, and gave it the name of *Undergraduate Papers,* with Nichol, of course, as editor. They scurried around until they found a publisher who agreed to publish and sell the magazine, and even to pay small sums to the contributors. All that the brotherhood of Old Mortality had to do was to get it written and ready for the press!

The young reformers soon found that they had not reckoned upon the inexorable demands of a printing press. All too soon what had started out as a labor of love became only labor; after the third issue the members of Old Mortality ran out of enthusiasm. Editor Nichol, faced with the stern necessity of preparing for examinations for his degree in April, 1858, found that his editorial duties demanded more of his time than he could spare. *Undergraduate Papers,* in keeping with the name of the fraternity which had given it birth, expired quietly that spring.

II *The Influence of Rossetti*

Ironically, the greatest impact upon Swinburne at Oxford came from one who had no direct connection with the university—Dante Gabriel Rossetti, a London painter and poet. When Swinburne returned to Oxford from the Long Vacation in the fall of 1857, he found Rossetti there with Edward Burne-Jones, William Morris, and several other aspiring painters on a busman's holiday—painting murals on the walls of the Debating Hall of the new

Oxford Union Society building. Rossetti and the Pre-Raphaelites had been well advertised to Swinburne through Lady Trevelyan, whose enthusiasm for them and their movement was of long standing and had been enhanced by her acquaintance with John Ruskin and William Bell Scott. With understandable eagerness Swinburne soon bent his steps to the Debating Hall.

Of such magnitude was Rossetti's influence upon Swinburne that a clear understanding of him and his works would be impossible without an extensive knowledge of the Italian-Englishman and his peculiar ideas. And to comprehend Rossetti fully, it is necessary to understand Pre-Raphaelitism, a term now almost synonymous with Rossetti, and the "art for art's sake" philosophy which he combined with Pre-Raphaelitism to form his own personal and artistic philosophy. We shall, therefore, deal with him at length.

A conglomeration of currents and crosscurrents, of rules laid down but frequently transgressed, of moods and enthusiasms, of various meanings to various people, Pre-Raphaelitism is neither simple to explain nor easy to understand. It originated in the spirit of rebellion against the authority of the Royal Academy which animated Holman Hunt and John Everett Millais, two young English painters struggling to win recognition in London in 1848. In that *annus mirabilis,* rebellion of all sorts was in the air, and no one should wonder that two young Bohemians caught the virus. Their grievance against the Academy was that they thought it ridden with formalism and hidebound with worship of old masters and old rules.

Their prescription to cure the Academy's ills was fashioned by Hunt, who was serious, earnest, and something of a philosopher. With the zeal of an evangelist, he agreed with Ruskin that all art should serve to bring the Kingdom of Heaven a little closer to earth. The painter, therefore, should begin with a "moral subject," one which would impress the beholder with a moral interpretation of some aspect of life, and then strive to put it on canvas just as he saw it and with almost photographic accuracy of detail. This last point he emphasized. At any cost, art must be true to nature and evidence such truth by meticulous attention to detail. The application of this prescription, Hunt argued fervently, would restore art from its moribundity under the hands of the Academy practitioners to a new and vital resurgence in the world of men.

Rossetti entered the movement quite naturally, for he was Hunt's pupil. He had too much of the gay picaro in him to be willing to dedicate his life to the teaching of truth through painting, but he joined with alacrity because he was a natural rebel against any kind of authority. He threw himself into the cause with zeal and rounded up several new recruits for the lark, including his brother William Michael, not a painter at all.

Great was the joy of the rebels when in the first volume of *Modern Painters* they found Ruskin condemning Roman artists for studying Raphael and for using his rules and reproducing his faults, instead of studying nature as Raphael had. The faults Ruskin objected to in the imitators of Raphael were, as Hunt saw them, precisely those of the Royal Academicians—the unnatural painting of figures, a slavish adherence to the outworn rules and methods of the "grand style," a false rendering of anatomy, a general disregard for truth, and an almost complete oblivion to the fundamental obligation of the artist to interpret the moral meaning of the life about him. Eagerly the English rebels adopted Ruskin's thesis and the name "Pre-Raphaelites," to which Rossetti suggested they add "brotherhood" as a token of the dedicated nature of their cause. So the Pre-Raphaelite Brotherhood came into being; the members swore secrecy and signed their pictures with the initials "PRB" after their names, more with a boyish desire to mystify the public than for any good reason.

So far, so good. But trouble came their way when, in 1850, Rossetti broke the oath of secrecy to let out of the bag the meaning of the initials and the purpose of the Brotherhood. Fully apprised of what these upstarts were about, the Academy rose in wrath and summoned to its aid the weight of authority and numbers. Because Hunt and Millais were better known, the full force of the tempest broke on their heads; but, by a quirk of criticism, Rossetti escaped almost completely and was even given a measure of praise in *The Times* for the poetry of his "Ecce Ancilla Domini." [3] To stem the tide, Millais succeeded in getting John Ruskin into the melee on the side of the Pre-Raphaelites on the ground that they were only practicing what he had taught. Even here the throw of dice was in Rossetti's favor, for, apparently hypnotized by Dante Gabriel's charm and air of authority, Ruskin hailed him as a Pre-Raphaelite chieftain and as an artist of outstanding merit.

The anger of Hunt and Millais at Rossetti for his betrayal of the secret meaning of "PRB" was all the greater when they saw him, a mere student, walking off with most of the honors and the chieftain's toga that should have gone to Hunt. But they were powerless to prevent it. With Ruskin's help and from a kind of natural magnetism from the Italianate connotations, the names "Dante Gabriel Rossetti" and "Pre-Raphaelite" became inextricably associated. Hunt and Millais felt certain that they had been cheated by that "sly Italian," as Millais' mother bitterly styled Rossetti, who, they were sure, had promoted his own interests at their expense.[4] Even though all the publicity had increased the popularity of all and raised the prices they could get for their pictures, the coolness among the three leaders grew so rapidly that the movement came to an end in 1852, at about the time the paper war against them subsided. By 1856 the Pre-Raphaelites had separated, each to follow his own pursuits.

Millais especially, though he rose to knighthood and the presidency of the Royal Academy, never forgave Rossetti. In 1896, though Rossetti had been dead fourteen years, Millais' rancor was still alive in his insistence that what Rossetti had practiced was not Pre-Raphaelitism: "His aims and ideals in art were also widely different from ours, and it was not long before he drifted away from us to follow his own peculiar fancies. What they were may be seen from his subsequent works. They were highly imaginative and original, and not without elements of beauty, but they were not Nature. At last, when he presented for our admiration the young women which have since become the type of Rossettianism, the public opened their eyes in amazement. 'And this,' they said, 'is Pre-Raphaelitism!' It was nothing of the sort. The Pre-Raphaelites had but one idea—to present on canvas what they saw in Nature; and such productions as these were absolutely foreign to the spirit of their work."[5]

This analysis holds more than a germ of truth. Though Rossetti's artistic principles and practices in many instances took their departure from Hunt's rationale of Pre-Raphaelitism, they departed so far that they became almost antithetical to the original. Hunt's insistence upon a moral purpose in theme and upon fidelity to truth in treatment meant nothing to Rossetti, who, as a complete Romantic in character and disposition, eschewed any form of discipline in life or painting. Much more fascinated was he with the emphasis of the Pre-Raphaelites upon the medieval scene and material which had come about through their absorption in the artists before Raphael, their adulation of Keats, and the widespread enthusiasm for things medieval in evidence on all sides in 1848, the Pre-Raphaelite natal year. Here Dante Gabriel was literally and figuratively at home. His enthusiasm for the Middle Ages was almost as old as his memory. The son of a Dante scholar, he had been brought up in a home haunted by the spirit of the great Florentine. The Dantesque influence was abetted by a boyhood love of Scott's novels which progressed to a later, even keener delight in the poetry of Keats, Browning, and Poe. From all these materials he created for himself a pseudo-medieval world of love, sin, and death—a world heavy with dark shadows and a sense of impending doom. Of course it was a world far removed from the real medieval world of history, but it was a world in which the neurotic Rossetti loved to dwell in fancy.

When Rossetti began to paint, quite naturally the pervasive influence of Dante and of the dream world which he—with Dante's help—had fashioned for himself flavored his works. No fewer than a dozen pictures are directly concerned with Dante or suggested by him, and the atmosphere and style are Dantesque. The paintings are heavy and dark, with little light; the faces are serious or sad, often in grief or pain, almost never with a smile or cheerful expression. The same dreamlike quality that hangs over the *Divine Comedy* marks Rossetti's paintings. They are steeped in a romantic ghostliness, a vagueness and unreality; and these qualities are achieved by the somber lighting, by the lack of sharpness and definiteness of line, and by the gloomy, tragic expressions on the faces.

A further departure from Pre-Raphaelitism came from Rossetti's almost psychotic sensuality. In real life he delighted in the role of Don Juan, and the procession of women who thronged through his life ranged from delicately spiritual Elizabeth Siddal to coarse, vulgar Fanny Cornforth.[6] Accordingly, in the greater number of his pictures woman is the center of interest. In compliance with Victorian taboos the women are always robed, but in such a way that more is often revealed than concealed. Invariably, too, the women are virginal and maidenly, with long, slender bodies; long, columnar necks; masses of luxuriant hair tumbling loosely about the shoulders; and sensitive, sensual mouths. Often he painted them with flowers—in their hair, or somewhere in the background—possibly a suggestion of virginity; but this virginity was waiting, expecting, yearning to be assailed. In accordance with Rossetti's observation that no woman is interesting until she has lost her virginity, he did pictures of some of the great prostitutes, adulterers, and adulteresses of history and legend: Rosamond, Lilith, Helen of Troy, Guinevere, Venus Astarte, Paolo and Francesca, and Tristram and Iseult.

By 1857, when Rossetti came to Oxford, he had added another ingredient to "Rossettianism," to borrow Millais' term. This ingredient was the idea that art had nothing to do with morality or moral didacticism and should be evaluated only on its merits as art. Diametrically opposed to the original Pre-Raphaelitism of Holman Hunt, this doctrine stemmed from Edgar Allan Poe's rebellion against the Victorian dictum that a poem should be judged by the moral truth it teaches. In this essay "The Poetic Principle," Poe states flatly that poetry should be evaluated only on its ability to excite and to elevate the soul. Such excitement and elevation are aroused, he maintains, only if the poem achieves real beauty. This attainment of beauty is the fundamental purpose of the poem, and any attempt to subordinate it to moral didacticism will inevitably militate against the creation of beauty.

Poe's essay was published in 1850, a year after his death. The idea was taken up in France by Théophile Gautier, who, in his book *Emaux et Camées* (1852), enunciates his version of Poe's theory, which he expresses as *l'art pour l'art,* or "art for art's sake." Influenced by Gautier, whom he called his "maître impeccable," Charles Baudelaire published a notable essay on Poe in 1852; and, because he was an art critic, he followed it with ample references to Poe's theory in his famous critiques, "Exposition Universelle de 1855" and "Salon de 1859." In the latter essay he paraphrases Poe by pointing out that a rigid adherence to truth is inimical to artistic beauty and by complaining that the French public demands truth where it should ask only for beauty in painting.[7] In the introductory essay, "Notes

Nouvelles sur Edgar Poe," to his translation of several of Poe's shorter works in his *Nouvelles Histoires Extraordinaires* (1857), Baudelaire—though he admits, as Poe did, that poetry might ennoble morals as a sort of by-product of its influence—insists that the prime aim of poetry must always be beauty. To attempt to make it subserve truth, science, or morality would prevent its attaining that sublime beauty which it must have if it is to elevate the human spirit to visions of the immortal and eternal—those beatific visions which Poe says are the ultimate goal of great poetry. Here, of course, is the aesthetic justification of "art for art's sake," just as the attainment of Heaven is the justification for religion. Only by serving art for the sole sake of art, say Poe, Gautier, and Baudelaire, can the faithful artist hope to create ideal beauty.

We pause here to point out, first, that Poe's idea was not completely original, for at least its essence is comprehended in Longinus' essay "On the Sublime," written in the first century A.D. Second, the great weakness of "art for art's sake" is that it is essentially Romantic and therefore essentially subjective. Divorced from Classicism or any other set of objective rules or principles, it trusts entirely to the artist's aesthetic tastes and perceptions to guide him in the search for and the creation of ideal beauty. However, if the artist is in any way abnormal, his artistic vision may likewise be distorted and may lead him far astray. So it was with Poe, whose fascination with the horrible often led him into morbidity. So it was with Gautier, who blended fantasy and the macabre to create the paganism of *Mademoiselle de Maupin,* the sensuality of *La Toison d'or,* the emphasis upon external beauty and workmanship and the indifference to morality of *Emaux et Camées.* So it was with Baudelaire, whose personal life of debauchery and taste for the erotic in art resulted in *Les Fleurs du Mal.* And so it was with Dante Gabriel Rossetti, who, hating all rules and discipline, leading a licentious and amoral life, and scorning all interference with his pleasure, was a "natural" for the new philosophy.

We do not know precisely how early Dante Gabriel embraced "art for art's sake" and added it to his peculiar brand of Pre-Raphaelitism. It could well have been in 1855, when he visited the Universal Exposition in Paris, in which Hunt and Millais were exhibiting, and for which Baudelaire wrote his famous

critique with frequent mention of Poe and with liberal paraphrases from Poe's "The Poetic Principle." Rossetti had a sharp
eye for anything new and significant in art or literature. Like
most English painters, he kept abreast of what was going on in
the art world of Paris. He could hardly have missed the essays
of Gautier and Baudelaire with their interesting affirmations of
the new philosophy. And, since Rossetti was a devotee of Poe,
claiming that he had written "The Blessed Damozel" as a companion piece to Poe's "The Raven," he could have read Poe's
essay as early as 1850 when it was first published. He could
have formed his first acquaintance with the essence of "art
for art's sake" then. Certainly, by the time he went to Oxford
in 1857, Rossetti was an enthusiastic follower of the new philosophy.

A third point to bear in mind about "art for art's sake" is that
Gautier, Baudelaire, and Rossetti did not confine it to their
practice of the arts but carried it over into their personal lives.
They did not say so, of course, but their reasoning obviously
went like this: if the work of art is to be free from moral standards and values, why should the artist not also be unfettered
by them? If his intuitions and his visions of beauty are to be his
only guides in art, why should they not guide him in life also?
In other words, why should he not be free to do as he wishes
both in art and life?

In this connection we must remember that "art for art's sake"
sprang from a rebellion against an overemphasized morality and
against the philosophy of Utilitarianism, represented in England
and America by the smug portrait of Queen Victoria; and
in France by the ubiquitous image of Napoleon III. In the
lengthy "Author's Preface" to his novel *Mademoiselle Maupin*
in 1834, long before he read Poe's essay and adopted "art for
art's sake," Gautier attacks Utilitarianism: "There is nothing
truly beautiful but that which can never be of any use whatso-
ever; everything useful is ugly, for it is the expression of some
need, and man's needs are ignoble and disgusting like his own
poor and infirm nature. The most useful place in a house is the
water-closet." [8] Even more far-reaching is Baudelaire's attack in
his "Notes Nouvelles sur Edgar Poe" upon those who reason
that because man is born good, his art should also be morally
good. All men are not born good, Baudelaire insists, with his

eyes upon some of the more macabre short stories of Poe; they are also born marked with evil, and it is both the privilege and duty of the artist to deal with this Satanic side of man and to express its beauty. Baudelaire's illustration of his own belief in the evil side of man is *The Flowers of Evil*, his book of poems first published in 1857, the same year as his essay on Poe.

Here again, of course, was justification for the artist personally to explore evil if he wished. Indeed, how could he portray it in art unless he thoroughly understood it? And how could he understand it unless he had experienced it in his own life? As we have noted, Gautier, Baudelaire, and Rossetti lived in open defiance of accepted moral standards and practices. As we have likewise noted, all three delved into the sensual, the animal, the abnormal sides of man's nature and presented them in connection with their work in painting, in literature, or in both. In Rossetti's case, the Satanic side of "art for art's sake" was ample justification for that medieval world of love, sin, and death that he created for himself, and for such paintings as "Bocca Bacciata" ("the kissed mouth") and "Found," the study of a London prostitute in her moment of greatest shame and agony. In his poetry he practiced the same philosophy in "Jenny," a compassionless meditation upon the life and character of a prostitute; in some of the more sensual sonnets of "The House of Life" cycle; in "Troy Town," a study of the pathological hatred of a scorned woman for her former lover; and in "The King's Tragedy," a study of murder and revenge. As in his painting, he had to be careful to disguise his real purpose from the ever-watchful and suspicious British Philistines. Britain was considerably less tolerant on moral grounds than was France, and Baudelaire's *Les Fleurs* was condemned by the French courts for immorality in 1856 and its author fined. Better, then, for Rossetti to go slow about publishing his poetry, and not to divulge his philosophy of art and literature beyond the circle of his immediate friends. Better to placate the British lion than to anger him; but, of course, if one could placate him by an apparent submission to his wishes while in reality one was slyly flaunting him and his absurd commands—why, all the better.

Besides being a painter and a poet, Rossetti was also an artist at befooling the British public. Sensing that the English inferiority complex toward Italian art and artists could be turned to the advantage of a clever Italian seeking to make his way in the arts, he rearranged his name from the baptismal Gabriel Charles Dante Rossetti to Dante Gabriel Rossetti. This was a shrewd move because it emphasized his Italianism and gave him a first name with the highest possible Italian literary connotations. Significantly, however, his family and close friends continued to call him "Gabriel" until his death and thus to write of him privately and publicly during his lifetime and after. His second step was to accent the Italianate in his appearance. Here nature aided him, for though he was one-quarter English, he was short in stature, inclined to be stout; he also had a swarthy complexion; heavy dark eyebrows over large, liquid dark eyes; and even in his late twenties a receding hairline that made him look ten years older. To these characteristics he added a heavy, drooping moustache and a chin-and-neck beard.

This was the man who, with a group of his young disciples he had gathered for the purpose, journeyed to Oxford to paint murals in the new Union building and whom Swinburne found there when he returned for the fall term. A good deal of "gush" has been written about the meeting between Swinburne and Rossetti. Some biographers of both treat it with awe and wonder, as though the heavens should have opened and prophetic voices been heard. They insist that Rossetti recognized almost instantly the genius in Swinburne and with admirable altruism determined to do all in his power to aid its development. What he actually saw before him was that which must have moved him to amazement first and then to silent laughter—an elfish little fellow five feet, four inches tall, of twenty who looked more like sixteen. If Rossetti did not know at the outset, he must have soon learned that Swinburne was of a wealthy, noble family—intelligence which would prick up his ears at the prospect of "tin," as he laughingly referred to money.

In short order Rossetti divined that he had in Swinburne a creature who was at the opposite sexual pole from himself. Whether Rossetti told the others we do not know, but he led the way in a program of jest and allusion at Swinburne's expense which must have been hard to take. In a letter to Rossetti in 1869, Swinburne outlined his plan for his *Tristram and Iseult* by detailing how Tristram would lay the groundwork for Iseult's seduction through tales of the sexual irregularities of other members of the

Court: ". . . but delicately, sparing respectfully the innocence of her who was to make the first and greatest scandal there of all in time—as in days past at Oxford, when we first met, you fellows might have respected my spotless adolescence. I don't say that you did." [9]

The effect of meeting Rossetti and his troupe of artists—William Morris, Edward Burne-Jones, Val Prinsep, and others—was electric. Swinburne was enchanted and lifted out of himself like the children of Hamelin when they first heard the fairy music of the Pied Piper. By this time he was surely aware that he was radically different from other young men. And he was filled with secret longings and desires that he had suppressed with shame because they were diametrically opposed to everything he had been taught. But here was a man with a philosophy that not only removed the shame, but encouraged him to express the longings and desires—in other words, to dare to be completely himself.

Not only the philosophy, but the man, too, fascinated Swinburne as no other ever had. Rossetti, had he wished, could certainly have been a great teacher. He had a hypnotic quality that made young men his devoted slaves and enabled him almost effortlessly and with a few words to so inspire them that the entire course of their lives would be changed. Burne-Jones, an Oxonian who also succumbed to Rossetti's charm, explained the effect of Rossetti's magic personality in an account that may well stand for Swinburne also:

He taught me to have no fear or shame of my own ideas, to design perpetually, to seek no popularity, to be altogether myself—and this not in any words I can remember, but in the tenor of his conversation always and in the spirit of everything he said. I remember that he discouraged me from study of the antique—the classical antique—giving as his reason that such study came too early in a man's life and was apt to crush out his individuality. . . . So what I chiefly gained from him was not to be afraid of myself, but to do the thing I liked most: but in those first years I never wanted to think but as he thought, and all he did and said fitted me through and through. He never harangued or persuaded, but had a gift of saying things authoritatively and not as the Scribes, such as I have never heard in any man.[10]

The phrases "taught me to have no fear or shame of my own ideas," "to be altogether myself," "to do the thing I liked most" all indicate that Rossetti preached the gospel of "art for art's sake" to his young followers. Swinburne's own testimony shows conclusively that his indoctrination into the new doctrine was by Rossetti. In a letter on October 9, 1866, to William Michael Rossetti, Swinburne explains why he ceased writing poetry in 1860 and 1861 to aid the cause of Italian liberty: ". . . it is nice to have something to love and to believe in as I do in Italy. It was only Gabriel and his followers in art (l'art pour l'art) who for a time frightened me from speaking out. . . ." [11] Later, referring to his unfavorable review of Hugo's *Les Miserables* in 1862, he says: ". . . I was just at that time . . . too much under the morally identical influence of Gabriel Gautier and of Théophile Rossetti not to regret . . . that a work of imagination should be coloured or discoloured by philanthropy, and shaped or distorted by a purpose." [12] The interchange of the given names of the two men is meant to emphasize the similarity of their influence.

Altogether, though Rossetti certainly gave Swinburne's literary creativity a decided stimulus, his influence was hardly the sort that a modern psychiatrist would have wished for him at this stage of his development. Rossetti and his thralls left Oxford by Easter, 1858—they never did finish the murals—but Swinburne made visits to London to sit at the feet of the maestro. To the neglect of his studies, the young Oxonian threw himself into the writing of poems and dramas dealing with medieval lore and imitative of those of Rossetti and Morris. With increasing boldness he gave vent to the abnormal promptings of his nature. By the end of 1859 he was giving so much time to writing poetry that he was in scholastic trouble. As a penalty for failing in examinations, he was rusticated in the early part of 1860. In June, 1860, he left the university for good without taking a degree and under mysterious circumstances which have never been cleared up. Jowett placed the blame on the Pre-Raphaelites. With greater precision he could have laid it squarely on the shoulders of the Pied Piper, Dante Gabriel Rossetti.

CHAPTER 3

The Oxford Litterateur

S WINBURNE'S OXFORD writings show very clearly his remarkable susceptibility to the influences upon him during
these four and a half years. He was a complete romantic, and
what he encountered in life, if it moved him emotionally and im-
pinged upon his consciousness, was quite certain to come out in
his writings. It is easy to discern the influence of Nichol and Old
Mortality, of Oxford Classicism, of his readings in Hugo and Balzac. But Swinburne's much more profound reaction to Rossettian
Pre-Raphaelitism and aestheticism is inescapable. The Oxford
writings show him carried away with an unrestrained enthusiasm.

The Oxford works exhibit also many of the defects that mar the
later works: the excessive delight in literary combat and the use
of invective; the unreasoning, uncompromising hatred of religion;
and the traces of sexual and psychological abnormality, together
with an increasing boldness in giving free rein to the expression
of his secret longings and desires—a boldness which, as we have
noted, was the direct result of his conversion to "art for art's sake."
Evident also in these writings of young manhood are the unmistakable signs of poetic genius and of the growth of technical skill
and lyrical power. By no means was Swinburne a full-fledged
poet when he left Oxford in June, 1860, but he was well on the
way to becoming one.

I *Italian Freedom*

Swinburne's interest in Italy was intensified at Oxford through
his contacts with Aurelio Saffi, lecturer at the Taylorean Institute,
the Oxford center for modern language study. This former associate of Mazzini, an exile from Italy since 1849, was a firsthand
source of information about the problems and troubles of Italy as
well as the activities of Mazzini and the revolutionary party then

struggling to throw off the yoke of the tyrants. Also through the young poet's adulation for Shelley and his enthusiasm for the poems of Browning, Italy had a claim upon his sympathy. The influence of Old Mortality raised his enthusiasm to a militant pitch.

Because it was always easier for Swinburne to hate than to love, his interest in Italian freedom centered on Ferdinand II, the Bourbon King of Naples, whose narrow escape from assassination in December, 1856, called the attention of the world to his tyrannical oppression of the people. In the essay "On Foreign Intervention," written in 1857-58 to be read before Old Mortality, Swinburne argued that, under extreme conditions, it was fitting and proper for one nation to interfere in the internal affairs of another. Ferdinand, he said, had created such intolerable conditions by treacherously abolishing the constitution and by doing all manner of injustices to the people, including imprisonment without trial of any who opposed him.[1]

Even more vitriolic is the attack upon Ferdinand in the "Ode to Mazzini," written in 1856-57. Stigmatizing Ferdinand as "the crowned serpent, skilled in many a wile,"[2] Swinburne asks passionately in accents that owe much to Hugo's *Les Châtiments* and to Shelley's "Ode to Naples":

> *Shrinks not thy soul before the shame it braves,*
> *The gathered anger of a patient land,*
> *The loathing scorn that hardly bears to name thee?*[3]

Austria is anathematized for her share in causing Italian woes, but the secret villain—the behind-the-scenes plotter who connives at and abets the tyranny—is the head of the Church of Rome. Italy must bear the curse of slavery because she has remained in spiritual bondage to the Pope. Swinburne urges her to cast off the yoke of Catholicism so as to stand untrammeled and ready when the day of freedom dawns.

Despite its obvious faults and its imitativeness of Hugo and Shelley, the "Ode to Mazzini" is a remarkable achievement for a young collegian at the beginning of his sophomore year. Swinburne never published it, possibly because, conscious of the synthetic quality of the emotion which produced it, he considered it unworthy of the subject.

[51]

The second Italian poem, "The Temple of Janus," was camouflaged as a Roman poem. Written for the Newdigate Prize in 1857, both the subject and the rhymed couplet style were dictated by the rules of the contest. Even so, Swinburne cleverly managed to get in his licks for the cause of Italian liberty.

Janus was the Roman god whose duty it was to guard the gates of the city and the portals of the home. Depicted as two-faced, he shows his alertness by simultaneously looking both behind and before. Swinburne used this characteristic to plan his poem as a backward glance at the glories of the free Roman Republic, a present look at the slavery of Italy under the "crowned snake of Naples," and a forward vision of the same advent of freedom which he had prophesied in the "Ode to Mazzini."

The overall length of the poem is about four hundred lines. So long a poem in rhymed couplets in any but the most skillful hands would have inevitably produced a soporific monotony. But here again Swinburne exhibits a cleverness that is remarkable. He secures variety by inserting an occasional triplet and by closing the stanzas with Alexandrines; even more effective are the bursts of turbulent lyricism that are not Dryden, nor Pope, nor even Shelley. They are pure Swinburne.

What fault the judges found with this poem, we do not know. Such contests often produce strange results, and this apparently was one of them. Swinburne was passed over in favor of a student named Worley, whose only claim to fame is this coincidental connection with a great poet. Possibly the judges were of Tory leanings and did not enjoy the emphasis on liberty or the condemnation of kings and priests. Possibly, too, their classical ears were so attuned to the ponderous beat of eighteenth-century rhymed couplets that Swinburne's tripping rhythms and bursts of fairy music bewildered and alienated them.

The third and last of the Italian poems—until he returned to the theme in 1866—was "The Ride from Milan," written in honor of the obscure battle of Melegnano, fought on June 8, 1858, shortly before the much greater victory of Magenta, with which Swinburne may have confused it. Chiefly interesting because it shows that the Pre-Raphaelite influence had not completely uprooted his devotion to Italian freedom, it still marks a considerable lessening of his zeal. Sincerity is lacking, and the poem is more of a prosodic exercise than the vehicle of a powerful emotion. The center of emphasis is the rhythm and rhyme, exactly those of Poe's "The Raven," a poem which may have been brought to his attention by Rossetti, long one of Poe's admirers. Present also for the first time is an overdose of alliteration and an unfortunate diction that at times verges on absurdity.

A good argument could be made for including the Italian poems as a subdivision of the works done under the influence of Old Mortality. They are at least partially a product of the republican spirit fanned into flame by Nichol and his group; but, because Swinburne's interest in Italy and her problems antedates his coming to Oxford, a separate grouping is perhaps more appropriate.

II *Republicanism*

Actually, if we except the Italian poems, the only one of the Oxford pieces to result directly from the influence of Nichol and Old Mortality was the essay "Church Imperialism," and even this can be attributed partially to the effect upon Swinburne of Hugo's *Les Châtiments.* Appearing in March, 1858, in the third number of the *Undergraduate Papers,* this is at once an attack upon Napoleon III of France and an appeal to Roman Catholics everywhere not to follow the lead of the Pope in supporting Napoleon. Otherwise, Swinburne warns, the Catholic Church would be gravely injured, and such an outcome would be "an injury to all men."

His hatred of the French Emperor is genuine enough. After Orsini's abortive attempt to assassinate Napoleon III, Swinburne hung Orsini's picture beside that of Mazzini on the wall of his room, going through an almost daily ritual of dancing and bowing before them.

III *Pre-Raphaelitism*

Far and away the larger portion of Swinburne's writings at Oxford bear the unmistakable impress of Pre-Raphaelite influence. On November 10, 1857, only nine days after his first encounter with the Pre-Raphaelites, he was engaged in writing his *Queen Iseult,* his first Pre-Raphaelite work.[4] Though he had intended to complete the poem in ten cantos, he broke it off at the beginning of the seventh and left it unfinished, disparaging it later as "some awful doggerel on the subject of Tristram and Iseult."[5]

Inspired by Morris's "Defence of Guinevere," the "Haystack in the Floods," and possibly by "The Battle of Crecy," *Queen Iseult* runs to 1,103 verses and is Swinburne's most sustained effort up to that time.

The poem begins with a lengthy and unnecessary account of the parentage, birth, and upbringing of Tristram, who, at twenty, journeys to Cornwall, reveals himself to his uncle King Mark, and is commissioned by him to go to Ireland for Yseult. What follows is largely the conventional story but with some noteworthy exceptions. When Tristram and Yseult arrive at King Mark's court, Tristram's qualms at continuing the affair with his uncle's wife while he is a guest in the uncle's palace are overcome by Yseult, who comes to him barefoot through the snow (why she was not wearing shoes is not made clear) and carries him on her back to her own room. And when they are finally discovered and exposed, Yseult, in a scene reminiscent of Morris' "Defence of Guinevere," outfaces King Mark before all his knights and boldly denies her guilt, saying that, if she had ever been unfaithful to him, it was with the same knight who had exposed her. Frustrated, Mark has to suffer the laughter of the knightly audience and to accept their verdict of her innocence, though he cannot rid himself of suspicion. Sorrowfully, Tristram leaves Cornwall and makes his way to Brittany, where he somewhat reluctantly weds another Yseult, described as "of the white hands" to distinguish her from Mark's wife, who is "of the yellow hair." Though the new Yseult loves him passionately, Tristram has only a paternal feeling for her; and, on their wedding night, he refrains from touching her. Back in Cornwall, she of the yellow hair mourns for him, comforting herself that, if he ever returns, he will find her older, but still golden haired and as much in love as ever.

In such absurdities as these it is not difficult to see the curious compound of Rossettian sensuality and aestheticism and the all too evident traces of Swinburne's abnormality. The result is altogether grotesque, for the two elements are as incompatible as oil and water. In Rossetti's pictures and poems, the lady's loose, flowing hair is a sensual symbol, and nothing more. But Swinburne makes Tristram ridiculous when he shows him willing to die for Yseult's hair, and has him exclaim, when he is absent from his lady, that he "thirsted for one tress." The abnormality also shows through the fear of sexual contact with women which is symptomatic of homosexuality. Such an unmasculine reaction is evidenced in Tristram's being so timid that the more aggressive Yseult has to carry him piggyback to her room. And, in the nuptial bed with Yseult of the white hands, the doughty knight trembles when she creeps close and asks him to kiss her. Weeping, he prays to God while she goes to sleep, puzzled and still a virgin.

The best feature of *Queen Iseult* is a compactness and economy of expression notable by its absence from Swinburne's later works. The scenes are vividly described; the mood and tone are sustained. Here and there the story comes to life with an immediacy that could have been created only by an imagination that lived the scenes as it created them.

Also strongly initiative of the Pre-Raphaelite interest in the medieval are such poems as "Lancelot," which shows the knight torn between his conscience and his adulterous love for Guinevere; the fragment "King Ban," dealing with Lancelot's parents; and the "Rudel" poems, three short poems about the love of the medieval troubadour Jaufre Rudel for the Countess of Tripoli.

The poem "The Queen's Tragedy," written in 1859, is of special interest. The unnamed queen, who narrates the story, tells to the maids who hold her arms while she lies in bed the grim story of how the king and her baby were murdered by cruel men. Heartbroken, she relives the story of how they killed her husband, cut off his head, and nailed it to the city walls. Despite her pleas that she is not mad and that she will not harm herself if they free her arms, her ravings show her derangement. As the poem closes, she fancies the king is again by her side; and she promises that, if he will love her again as he did when they first met, she will blossom as beautifully and sing as sweetly as she did then.

If we place this poem beside Rossetti's "The King's Tragedy," completed in March, 1881, and published later that year,[6] the mystery of the identity of the king and queen is solved. Rossetti tells the story of the murder of James I of Scotland at the Charterhouse in Perth in 1437 by Robert Graeme and his men, despite the heroic efforts of his queen, the former Jane Beaufort, daughter of the Earl of Somerset and of Catherine Douglas, to save him. After the deed, the murderers flee to the Highlands before the king's men can seize them. Although the murder takes place in February, the queen keeps the king's body lying in state in Charterhouse Chapel till nearly the end of March, when the last wretch is caught and hanged.

Rossetti paints a vivid picture of the queen sitting and praying beside the bier all those weeks, giving no sign to anybody except Catherine Douglas. As Catherine brings her the news, the queen's face grows livid as she leans over and whispers to the dead king the name of the traitor punished. She falls to the floor with froth on her lips when the name is that of the arch-traitor, Sir Robert Graeme. After the last traitor is hanged, she rises from her grim vigil, withered and wasted by her grief.

Swinburne's poem takes up the tale at this point, showing the queen's last haunted hour, her mind unsettled by grief and despair, doubtful of God's existence or mercy, yearning to be reunited with her murdered husband. We must admit that Swinburne's tragedy is not a tragedy as it stands, because the reader is not acquainted with the details necessary to establish the tragic thesis. Nor, for this same reason, as well as for the fact that the audience is never clearly described or permitted to become part of the scene, is it a good dramatic monologue.

Whose was the original inspiration to use this material—Rossetti's or Swinburne's? Because Swinburne wrote his poem twenty-two years before Rossetti, and because Scottish history and legend were much closer to him—"Capheaton" was only a few miles from the Border—than to Rossetti, he is the more likely choice. The reasonable conjecture is that Swinburne, during one of his frequent visits to London in 1859 and 1860, read his poem to Rossetti after first briefing him on the details leading up to the murder. Rossetti then filed the details, including the title, away in his memory, and resurrected them in 1880-1881 for "The King's Tragedy."

He should, of course, have given Swinburne proper credit. But he had completely broken off his friendship with Swinburne in 1872; and if his conscience gave him even a momentary twinge, he could have eased it by reflecting that he had used only that part of the material that Swinburne had not included, and that Swinburne had never deemed "The Queen's Tragedy" worthy of publication. The incident serves to show, however, that whatever the benefits were that may have attended the friendship of the

two men, they were not always flowing in one direction. Rossetti
did learn some things from the brilliant young Oxonian.

In an entirely different vein from "The Queen's Tragedy" are
the seven sonnets that T. J. Wise titled "Undergraduate Sonnets"
and published after Swinburne's death. Scholars have always
considered them a mere poetic exercise, partly in imitation of
Shakespeare (whose prosody they follow) and partly of Rossetti,
whose translation of Dante's *Vita Nuova* sonnets led him to
adopt the sonnet as one of his favorite verse forms. Swinburnians
have always believed that the poet's love affair was with "Boo"
Faulkner, the adopted daughter of London friends, whom he
met in 1862 or 1863. But in 1858 Professor Cecil Y. Lang published an article containing the argument that Swinburne's passion was not for "Boo" at all—she was only ten in 1863—but
for his cousin Mary Gordon.[7] My feeling is that the emotion was
real and that the sonnets were probably written to Mary Gordon.
Since she was only three years his junior and since they had
been thrown together since childhood, he could well have been
in love with her while he was at Oxford; or, another possibility,
the sonnets might well have been written at any time after Swinburne left Oxford until the spring, 1864, when Mary Gordon
apparently rejected him in favor of another.

IV *Miscellaneous Poems*

During the Oxford years Swinburne tried his hand at a wide
variety of poetic forms and subjects, ranging from translations
of Dante and Villon to ballads in imitation of the Border Ballads, a translation of the Catholic chant *Dies Irae,* and two
sonnets titled "The Cup of God's Wrath," paraphrases of Biblical
material. Since these are imitations and nothing more, there is
no necessity for dealing with them at length.

Even less worthy of attention is the poem "The Death of
Sir John Franklin" which Swinburne wrote in two mornings of
February, 1860, while he was in rustication with the Reverend
Stubbs of Navestock. A poem of about two hundred lines, it was
written for a special prize of £50 for the best poem on the life,
death, and character of Sir John Franklin, the explorer who had
perished on an Arctic expedition. The result was a tedious poem
in iambic pentameter with a loose rhyme scheme. We cannot
escape the suspicion that Swinburne was more interested in the

£50 than in Sir John, for this is a mere poetic exercise like "The Triumph of Gloriana" of Eton days. As in the case of "The Temple of Janus," Swinburne saw the prize go to another. That Swinburne's offering dealt only with Franklin's death, to the exclusion of his life and character, and that its author had already departed Oxford under questionable circumstances may have cost him the victory.

V *The Dramas*

The active interest in the Elizabethan drama Swinburne displayed even before he went to Eton continued and grew stronger during the Oxford years, intensified to some degree by Pre-Raphaelite archaism and medievalism, even though the Pre-Raphaelites themselves had little interest in the drama as an art form. The result was three drama fragments—*The Laws of Corinth, Laugh and Lie Down,* and *The Loyal Servant*—all in the Elizabethan style and heavily indebted to Elizabethan plays and playwrights. The first of these, *The Laws of Corinth*—written in 1858 in imitation of *The Old Law* of Massinger and Middleton with some stylistic borrowings from Beaumont, Fletcher, and Chapman—is a fragment of one act and part of a second which centers around the love of Philocles, nephew of King Lysader of Corinth, for Erota, daughter of the aristocrat Antigonus. It is a maze of plot and counterplot told with such ranting and pseudo-Elizabethan fustian that we cannot regret that Swinburne carried this extravaganza no further.

To the second fragment, *Laugh and Lie Down,* Swinburne referred in a letter to a friend in 1874: "I suppose you can tell me nothing . . . of the *other* comedy attributed to C. T. [Cyril Tourneur] by Lowndes, with the charming title of 'Laugh and Lie Down.' I was so delighted with the name that in my last Oxford year I wrote in three days three acts of a comedy, after (a long way after) the late manner of Fletcher, under that title; but I shall take good care that this one never sees the light!" [8]

The nature of this fragment, written in 1859 and still unpublished, reveals clearly why Swinburne resolved to keep it hidden. Replete with flagellation resulting from abnormalities of love and sex, with uncertainties and mixtures of sex in which a man falls in love with a boy dressed as a girl, and with the question of another individual who may be a hermaphrodite, the play shows to what degree Swinburne gave free rein to his abnormal longings under the new freedom urged upon him by Rossetti, Pre-Raphaelitism, and aestheticism. As it stands, the play is a psychiatric document—a most significant item in a case history that leaves little room for reasonable doubt of one aspect of Swinburne's abnormality. Here, for instance, is the scene in which the page boy Frank confesses his love for his cruel mistress, the beautiful courtesan Imperia:

> Imperia.   *I tell you, if you use me lovingly,*
>   *I shall have you whipt again, most pitifully whipt*
>   *You little piece of love.*
> Frank.   *God knows I care not*
>   *So I may stand and play to you, and you kiss me*
>   *As you used to kiss me tender little side-touches*
>   *Of your lip's edge i' the neck.*
> Imperia.   *By my hand's hope,*
>   *Which is the neck of my lord Galeas,*
>   *I'll love your beard one day; get you a beard, Frank;*
>   *I were as well love a maid as you*
>   *With such a child's cheeks.*
> Frank.   *Madam, you have pleasant hands,*
>   *What sweet and kissing colour goes in them*
>   *Running like blood. . . .*
>
>   · · · · · · · · · · · · ·
>
>   *What makes you sigh still? You are now*
>   *So kind the sweetness in you stabs mine eyes*
>   *With sharp tears through.* I would so fain be hurt
>   But really hurt, hurt deadly, to do good
>   *To your most sudden fancy.*[9]

The Loyal Servant, the last of the Oxford dramas and the most nearly complete of them all, consists of four full acts and the first scenes of the fifth. Probably written toward the end of 1859 and the beginning of 1860, it contributed in good measure to the academic disaster which ended Swinburne's Oxford career. It represents a backward turn in his dramatic development rather than a step forward; for, where the plot was original

and the diction modern in *Laugh and Lie Down*, this play
closely follows the plot of Marston's *Anthony and Mellida* and
the dialogue is so affectedly archaic that it verges on absurdity.

VI *Literary Criticism*

In 1857 and 1858 Swinburne appeared also as literary polem-
icist and critic, the third of the roles he was to assume in his
later career. Ordinarily, we would not amalgamate these two
functions and designate them as one role, but in Swinburne's
case criticism was inevitably and inextricably mixed up with
polemics. It was also intertwined with his emotions, his likes
and dislikes. Even when he set out to praise unstintedly the
works of some friend, he rarely did so without giving some
backhanded blows by drawing invidious comparisons to others
he disliked. Thus in his *Notes on Poems and Reviews* (1866)
he defended his own poems and sneered at those of Robert
Buchanan. In his *Fortnightly Review* eulogy of Rossetti's
Poems (1870) he found Rossetti's verse superior in religious
sincerity to that of Robert Browning and Cardinal Newman.
In his *Fortnightly Review* article, "Mr. Arnold's New Poems"
(October, 1867), he lauded Arnold and disparaged David Gray.
And he extravagantly praised the novels of Charlotte Bronte as
greatly superior to those of George Eliot in his essay, "A Note on
Charlotte Bronte" (1877).

This trait is evident in the first piece of published criticism
he wrote, the article on Congreve in 1857 for the *Imperial Dic-
tionary of Universal Biography*. After praising the sharpness
and clearness of Congreve's mind, he says: "There is more
weight and matter in Congreve than in any English Dramatist
since the Restoration and at worst he is no coarser than his
time. . . . As a comic writer he stands above the best who came
after him, and beside the best who went before." [10] Now there
is nothing intentionally polemical in these remarks, nor would
they be likely to raise animosities when the writers who might
have been offended by them were all dead at least a half century. But later on, when Swinburne drew similar invidious
comparisons between living men of letters, ire and bitter recrim-
inations were the usual result.

This comparative method is used in another early article,

"The Early English Dramatists," published in December, 1857, in the first number of the *Undergraduate Papers*. In it he is comparing Marlowe and Webster, whom he finds similar in their ability to plumb the profundities of human character, in their command of language, and in their abhorrence of insincerity. This essay is noteworthy because, only a few weeks after meeting the Pre-Raphaelites, he shows the impact of Pre-Raphaelitism in his praise of Marlowe and Webster for their adherence to nature. "Their style," he says, "has the simple and noble outlines of the great early painters of Italy and Flanders." [11]

Both the Congreve article and the essay on Marlowe and Webster are gentleness itself compared to the third essay, "Modern Hellenism," an attack on Matthew Arnold which appeared in the second number of the *Undergraduate Papers* in January, 1858. This one is Swinburne with his fangs bared. He takes exception to remarks Arnold had made in a lecture in the Oxford Theatre to the effect that the Athenians of the Age of Pericles were a more cultured and refined lot than the English in the Elizabethan times, and that, specifically, Sophocles and Thucydides were superior to Sir Walter Raleigh. Waving the Union Jack, Swinburne sneers: "It may be that we have been hitherto mistaken; but we must have more than the measured rhetoric of a lecture to prove that we must resign the heroes of our own history for the idols of Oxford Hellenism." [12]

The last of the undergraduate attempts at criticism is a critical burlesque called "The Monomaniac's Tragedy," published in the second of the *Undergraduate Papers* in January, 1858, and never reprinted. Purportedly a review of the poems of Ernest Wheldrake, "author of Eve, a Mystery," this is the first of several such burlesques which Swinburne perpetrated in his later career and used to ridicule people and ideas that moved him to derisive laughter. In the "review" he pretends to quote excerpts from Wheldrake's poems, but they are, of course, his own. In these quotations he is evidently ridiculing the Spasmodic Poets and two of their leaders, Alexander Smith and Sydney Dobell. Like the Beatniks of the twentieth century, the Spasmodic Poets believed they first must woo the poetic mood or trance, and that what came forth then was inspired verse, regardless of its absurdities. Swinburne satirizes such extravagances by having Ernest Wheldrake commit a variety of crimes in order to secure material for poetry which, when it comes, pours forth in ranting:

> Oh! ah! oh!
> Ha! Ha! it burns me. Have I found him there?
> Nay, thou dead pain, it shall not alter thee;
> Tho' I hurled heaven into the reeling spume
> Of thunder-whitened ages, haled the moon
> At some red meteor's palpitating heels,
> A mangled residue of beams—what else? [13]

This parody is at once criticism and delicious humor. More effectively than a whole volume of criticism could, it exposes the faults of the Spasmodic philosophy and practice—faults which have today relegated the Spasmodic verse to the limbo of forgotten literature.

CHAPTER 4

Life for Art's Sake

SWINBURNE'S first problem, when he departed Oxford in June, 1860, was to win his father's approval to go to London to try his luck in the literary world. Admiral Swinburne's reluctance (he had retired from the Navy as a rear admiral in 1857) to endorse such a scheme is completely understandable. After all, Swinburne's academic debacle had been brought about by his suceptibility to the aestheticism of Rossetti and his Pre-Raphaelites. Why permit him to feed on more of the same?

By this time the Admiral must have had at least strong suspicions of his son's abnormality. If Lafourcade's conjecture is correct that Swinburne's giving free rein to his secret longings led to "bacchic excesses" which forced Oxford authorities to request his departure, at least for the time being, then Jowett would have known the full story.[1] And, if Jowett knew it, he would have been negligent in his duties not to have acquainted the Admiral with full particulars. Furthermore, Admiral Swinburne had been in the British Navy for about forty-seven years; inevitably, cases of sexual abnormality among seamen would have come to his attention; and, as an officer, he may have had to deal with them. At least the common symptoms of such cases would be familiar to him, and he could hardly fail to perceive them in Algernon, in whom they were quite evident.

So the Admiral's consent was slow in coming, but it did come. In the spring of 1861 he gave his reluctant approval and an annual allowance of £200 to set his son up at 16 Grafton Street in London. Evidently, Swinburne's father nourished hopes that his son's literary enthusiasms would wane and that he in time might be persuaded to make his peace with the authorities of Oxford and take his degree. In any case, the annual caution money to keep his name on the roll of students was paid till 1878, the year after the Admiral's death.[2]

The hopes were vain and the money wasted. Once launched on the town, Swinburne was off like an uncaged bird. After all, he was twenty-four in the spring of 1861, and for the first time in his life he was completely on his own and had happiness at last. The guns were firing on Fort Sumter across the Atlantic, but they raised not an echo of interest in the former apostle of freedom. Fears were abroad that Napoleon might attempt what his greater uncle had never been able to bring off—an invasion of Britain— but that, too, caused little concern in one who a year before had clamored for Napoleon's assassination. English interest in Italian liberty was at a high pitch all about him; Swinburne's interest was centered on his own freedom. Life was too exciting, too full of endless possibilities to bother about other people's woes.

His career in London for the next six years was at least as harmful and disreputable as the Admiral could have dreaded. All things conspired against Swinburne as though a malignant fate dominated his life. Three separate factors operated so as to carry him almost to mental, moral, and physical disaster. The first of these was the continued, bad influence of Dante Rossetti and of other persons whom Swinburne met through him. Second was the equally bad effect of close association with Richard Monckton Milnes (later Lord Houghton) and, through him, with several other men whose influence was strongly negative. Finally, Swinburne had to endure the shattering blow of being rejected in love by his cousin Mary Gordon, who, so far as we know, was the only girl for whom he ever felt the passion of love. The cumulative effect of three such handicaps would be difficult for even a strong individual to withstand; for Swinburne, they were well nigh catastrophic.

I *Rossetti's Disciple*

In seeking London and Rossetti, Swinburne was reacting in a pattern now quite familiar to modern psychiatrists. Those afflicted with homosexual leanings have a marked tendency to move to large centers of population, where they can follow their abnormal longings without the constant fear of detection that threatens in smaller communities.[3] Although the large number of Swinburnes and Ashburnhams living in and around, or traveling through London, created some hazards even there, the very size and character of London offered more anonymity, and perhaps illicit opportunity, than any other British city. Likewise, in attaching himself to Rossetti, he was only doing what he would be expected to do in his circumstances. The sexually abnormal male often seeks an idealized bond or relationship with an older man who, he feels, takes a real interest in him.[4] Although he may not be aware of his own motive, he is of course only attempting to compensate for the lack of a normal father-son relationship.

As we have seen, Rossetti was neither an idealist nor an altruist. Despite his surface glitter and his admitted genius, he had little capacity for friendship. He used people for his own ends, diverting their money and influence to his own benefit when he could—as in the case of Ruskin and Morris—then casting them aside when they rebelled. Except in a few cases, his friendships did not last long because, sooner or later, his victims became aware of what he was doing. He attracted and fascinated young men always, but, when they began to question his impositions or his authority, the end of their association was in sight. Always he traded upon youth; older men saw through him too soon and too clearly, and even the young ones soon grew restive under his domination. Of him Val Prinsep said: ". . . like the dread Jehovah of the Israelites, he was a jealous God, and, from the moment he was not all in all to us, a gradually widening rift established itself." [5] To put it bluntly, Rossetti was pretty hard to take over the long pull, and anybody with spirit refused to put up with him.

Swinburne, however, was so bedazzled with hero worship that he saw no blemish in his idol. One of Hadji's weaknesses and virtues was that, where he gave friendship, he gave implicit and unquestioning trust. In return he expected the same generous friendship and trust. If in any way a supposed friend violated his high code of friendship, Swinburne's rage was fierce and unrelenting. So many betrayals did he suffer in the first half of his life, that he became increasingly suspicious and chary of friendship as he grew older. One of his greatest betrayals, he came to believe later, was at Rossetti's hands; and his bitterness toward the artist was commensurate with what his affection had been.

"And indeed the bonds between this poet and this painter were closer than any such statements can imply," says Ford Madox Hueffer of the friendship between Rossetti and Swinburne in the early 1860's.[6] At least they were from Swinburne's side. From Rossetti's? Rossetti had a cruel sense of humor which delighted to ridicule those under his spell. Swinburne had not been long in London when Rossetti asked him to pose with the voluptuous Fanny Cornforth for a picture which he promised would be used as the frontispiece for his anthology of translations entitled *The Early Italian Poets*. As Swinburne wrote Milnes on October 15, 1861, "Rossetti has just done a drawing of a female model and myself embracing—I need not say in the most fervent and abandoned style—meant for a frontispiece to his Italian translations. Two mornings of incessant labour on all hands completed the design; and the result will I suppose be, as everybody who knows me already salutes the likeness with a yell of recognition,—that when the book comes out I shall have no refuge but the grave." [7]

Biographers of Swinburne and Rossetti have always passed over this incident without comment, assuming, as Swinburne obviously did, that the picture was in good faith. Casting him in such a role was a mockery. Homosexuality is at least partially the result of secret, disabling fears of womankind;[8] the homosexual, therefore, shuns and dreads any close contact with members of the opposite sex outside his own family, a fact which so worldly a man as Rossetti must have known. Forcing poor Swinburne to remain in such a posture with Fanny Cornforth through most of two mornings was as diabolical a bit of torture as any ever devised during the Middle Ages.

This prank was not the last of its kind played on Swinburne by his beloved master. In 1867-1868, when the equestrienne Adah Isaacs Menken came to England, Rossetti urged her on Swinburne.[9] Rumor had it that he gave her £10 to seduce the poet and that she returned the money, confessing her failure. We wonder if he had made a like offer to Fanny to inspire her to her best efforts when she posed with Swinburne.

Such antics as these may have caused Swinburne some discomfort but hardly anything worse. Rossetti's Bohemian way of life, inculcated by precept and example during Swinburne's frequent visits to his studio in Chatham Place by Blackfriars Bridge and later at Tudor House did much more to Swinburne's moral fiber. Such visits became almost a daily occurrence after he went to London. It would have taken someone much more naïve than he not to have soon realized that the artist practiced in everyday life his philosophy of trusting his intuitions and impulses and of casting aside any and all inhibitions. With Rossetti, sexual expression was as necessary and natural as meat and drink, and it was treated as casually. It bothered him not a bit one day in 1852 to notify brother William Michael and Holman Hunt not to come to his rooms because Elizabeth Siddal was coming and he did not wish to be disturbed.[10] In the last years of his life he instructed Hall Caine not to leave his room and come down stairs when Mrs. Jane Morris was with him.[11]

Such restrictions were a necessary condition of friendship with Rossetti. As William Bell Scott puts it: All his close friends accepted "certain peculiarities in him. . . . placing him in a position different from themselves, a dangerous position to the man whose temperament takes advantage of it." [12] Following the usual pattern of Rossetti's friendships, Swinburne's affection for him cooled off appreciably in 1863 and 1864. After the suicide of Elizabeth Siddal Rossetti in 1862, Swinburne, Rossetti, and George Meredith went to live in Tudor House. In a relationship that left no room for doubt, Rossetti soon installed there the coarse Fanny Cornforth, whom Swinburne later referred to as "the bitch." [13] This was a "peculiarity" that Swinburne, who had a deep and abiding affection for Elizabeth Siddal Rossetti, could not accept. He soon moved out, and, though he and Rossetti continued to see each other occasionally, the old fealty was gone.

By that time, however, most of the damage to Swinburne was already done, but not all of it was the responsibility of Rossetti. Through him and those who orbited about him, Swinburne met several unsavory characters who helped along his deterioration. Among them were Burne-Jones, who encouraged his abnormal tendencies;[14] Simeon Solomon, the young Jewish painter who may have been introduced to him by Burne-Jones,[15] and who was or soon became a homosexual, for his letters to Swinburne indicate an abnormal relationship; Charles Augustus Howell, parasite, trickster, liar, and—according to William Rossetti's daughter, Helen Rossetti Angeli—one of several of Swinburne's friends who flogged him for his pleasure.[16] Through these men Swinburne met still other objectionables like John Camden Hotten, Savile Clark, and John Thomson, who was connected with and perhaps part owner of a sort of brothel in St. John's Wood, where Swinburne went in the late 1860's to be flogged by the beautiful and mysterious "Mrs. A." [17]

The induction into "art for art's sake" Rossetti had given Swinburne at Oxford was intensified and amplified after he came to London. In James McNeill Whistler, whom he probably met through Rossetti, he found a complete devotee of Gautier and Baudelaire. Having recently come from Paris, where he had been thoroughly immersed in the new philosophy, Whistler was an authority on both the theory and practice of the new doctrine. Swinburne was an inspired pupil. He broke into print as an apostle of the new artistic freedom on June 7, 1862, when his letter to the editor of the *Spectator,* replying to an unfavorable review of Meredith's *Modern Love, and Poems of the English Roadside* appeared in that journal. All schools of poetry, Swinburne argued, should not be circumscribed by "nursery walls," as the popular school of that day was. Any subject "worth the serious interest of men" should be treated in the adult fashion of the *Modern Love* sonnets.[18] He amplified and clarified his thesis in his review of Baudelaire's *Les Fleurs du Mal,* published first in 1857, later recalled and somewhat expurgated as the result of a lawsuit and fine of Baudelaire's French publisher. Republished in 1861, this was the subject of Swinburne's review in the *Spectator,* a magazine opened to him through Lord Houghton, who introduced him to editor Richard Holt Hutton, on September 6, 1862.[19]

In this article, the first important one in England on Baudelaire, Swinburne begins with a bold statement that art has nothing to do with morals or didacticism. Then, turning his attention to the verse, he praises it for the exquisite workmanship which "makes every subject admirable and respectable." [20] Warming to his subject, he goes a step further in praise of Baudelaire's philosophy of the beauty of evil. He finds the morbid subject matter of *Les Fleurs du Mal* fascinating because "It has the languid, lurid beauty of close and threatening weather—a heavy, heated temperature, with dangerous hot-house scents in it; thick shadow of cloud about it, and fire of molten light." [21] Even the most loathsome subjects, he finds, are made beautiful by the perfect art of the poet. Then he effects a synthesis of beauty and morality with a bold declaration that ". . . there is not one poem of the Fleurs du Mal which has not a distinct and vivid background of morality to it." [22] After quoting eighty-three lines from a number of poems, he completes the introduction of the British public to the French voluptuary by quoting from the "Litanies de Satan," which he acclaims "one of the noblest lyrics ever written." [23]

Swinburne's covert purpose in this article was to place the poems of the Frenchman before the British; his secondary object was to enunciate the principles of "art for art's sake" and to illustrate them forcibly from Baudelaire. Hence the too long and too many quotations from *Les Fleurs.* Hence, also, the farfetched equation of beauty with morality. (Even Baudelaire thought that Swinburne had gone too far in his praise, for he wrote the young enthusiast that he was not at all as much of a moralist as Swinburne seemed to believe.) [24] Swinburne's third purpose in this article was, of course, to execute a frontal attack upon British morality and religion. He did it deliberately and, I believe, with full awareness of what he was doing. Here he was going beyond his master, for though Rossetti practiced and lived according to "art for art's sake" and though he joked about the proprieties in private, he did not dare to do so openly.

To what extent Rossetti may have encouraged Swinburne to write this article, we can only conjecture. The painter was too enthusiastic a practitioner of the new gospel to have endeavored to dissuade him. The spectacle of a young Englishman of excellent family, educated in an English university, lauding a French pornographer and quoting his obscenities in a respectable English family magazine might well have appealed to Rossetti's cruel sense of humor. The fact that Swinburne was also presenting himself to his own people as a dangerous young man—something of a literary subversive who would bear watching—would have bothered Rossetti's conscience not at all.

In fairness to Rossetti, we may say that his influence on Swinburne was not wholly bad. Rossetti was a talented poet and a critic of no mean ability. In his early years in London Swinburne benefited considerably from Rossetti's criticism and inspiration. Even the bad influence Rossetti exerted upon Swinburne was not malicious. What he taught Swinburne was what he honestly believed and practiced himself, what he imparted to all his young disciples, Morris and Burne-Jones included. When he realized that Swinburne was carrying out his gospel so literally that his life was in danger, Rossetti was worried and perhaps conscience-stricken. But Swinburne's deterioration had gone so far, and Rossetti's influence over him had lessened to such a degree by 1865, that the painter was powerless to undo the harm he had caused.

II *Lord Houghton's Influence*

On the face of his position and his many accomplishments, we would expect Lord Houghton's influence on Swinburne to be good: politician, scholar, man of the world, biographer of Keats, patron of young men of genius, fellow student at Cambridge with Thackeray and Tennyson, social luminary, and *bon vivant* —here was a man with much to give in wisdom, experience, criticism, and influence to a talented young literary man trying to make his way in the world. But, alas, the total effect of Swinburne's relations with Lord Houghton was on the negative side. In fact, if Lord Houghton had deliberately planned to ruin Swinburne's character and reputation, he could hardly have done a more thorough piece of work.

Because he was older than Rossetti, held a much higher position of respectability in the world, and was a man from the same social class as the Swinburnes and the Ashburnhams, Lord Houghton's power for good or evil over Swinburne was nearly as great as the painter's. He lacked Rossetti's genius and personal magnetism, but he made up for it in his wide knowledge of the world and in his great personal influence. Swinburne could respect Rossetti as an artist, but he could never accept him as a social equal—and his unsavory way of life in his dingy studio was altogether another world from that of "East Dene" or "Capheaton." But Lord Houghton was widely known and respected as a friend of such people as Gladstone, Disraeli, Jowett, Carlyle, and Palmerston. Consequently, when Houghton gave his blessing to pornography or illicit sexuality, the effect upon his young friend was almost the same as if the Earl of Ashburnham or Admiral Charles Henry Swinburne had done so.

The harm Houghton did Swinburne was along three distinct but related lines of action. First, he intensified the young poet's abnormal sexuality by encouraging him to revel in pornography of all kinds and by placing in his hands books otherwise hard to obtain—like those of the Marquis de Sade. Many of these works dealt with flagellation, frequently a concomitant of homosexuality; many of the letters between Swinburne and Houghton show that the older man encouraged the younger one to dwell upon such subjects. Second, Houghton influenced Swinburne to write pornographic poetry and prose and to give full vent to aberrant sexual tendencies, not, as Rossetti had, under the pretext of serving art, but for the joy of such abnormalities. Third, Houghton took a perverse delight in exhibiting Swinburne and his most offensive poems before persons who would be most shocked by them, usually people of prominence and influence, so that Swinburne's reputation was considerably damaged in important quarters. Because of Swinburne's subscription to Baudelaire's philosophy of the beauty of evil and because of his own love of shocking, he was willing to be exhibited.

The date of his first meeting with Lord Houghton is uncertain, but it was probably in 1861. It could have been earlier, for both men belonged to the Hogarth Club as early as 1858. In any case, by 1861 they were on intimate terms. Within a few months, Houghton was entertaining Swinburne at his country home at Fryston, where his inordinate love of smut had led him to collect one of the largest libraries of erotica in the British Isles. Here he invited his especial guests and put into their hands the latest and juiciest titles gathered from all over Europe. So paradoxical was his nature that on one Sunday morning he paused long enough to point out to his guests the exact location of his worst books and then continued on his way to Fryston Church with Lady Houghton.[25]

We are aware that most men relish a salacious jest as long as it is clever and contains real humor. After all, such humor springs from man's rather laudable refusal to take himself too seriously; it is his philosophical laughter at his own earthiness and human frailty. And we freely admit that some of the supreme humor of all ages is contained in jokes about those areas of experience not properly mentioned in mixed company. But a wide gulf lies between humor and the sort of thing Lord Houghton delighted in: the writings of the Marquis de Sade, for instance, whom Anatole France called "notre fou." [26] Redolent of homosexuality and lust, they are the excretions of depravity, and only a depraved mind could find anything good in them.

The greatest single disservice Houghton did Swinburne was, therefore, to introduce him to de Sade's works, probably in August, 1862.[27] Outlawed in both France and England, de Sade's writings would be hard to find outside such a library as Houghton's, and for good reason. For instance, one of the worst of them is the "Dialogue entre un Prêtre et un Moribond," which combines unbridled lust and homosexuality with savage scorn and mockery of religion.

We can readily imagine Swinburne's delight in de Sade. This same intermingling of a denunciation of religion as hypocrisy and a reveling in abnormal sexuality was adopted by Swinburne and remained with him the rest of his life. One usually called forth the other, even in his private letters. More than any other factor, this obnoxious aspect of his poetry enraged the British public and brought down its wrath upon Swinburne in 1866.

That which fascinated Swinburne most in de Sade's works was the novel *Justine ou les Malheurs de la Vertu*. The story concerns Justine's trials and tortures at the hands of the homosexual Bressac and his valet, Jasmin. That she loves Bressac means nothing to him, nor does it temper the indignities he heaps upon her womanhood. He attacks and ridicules her religious beliefs, she being portrayed as quite devout. Perhaps the crowning atrocity of the novel occurs when Bressac puts a dagger into the hand of Justine and guides it into his mother's heart. *Justine* is crammed full of sadism, masochism, sodomy, incest, atheism, murder, and the same scorn of religion combined with abnormal lust that we noted in the "Dialogue." None of it was good pabulum for an erratic young fledgling only two years out of Oxford.

De Sade became an obsession with Swinburne and remained so until the end of his life. De Sade, whose very name is the root of the word *sadism,* and Lord Houghton brought out the very worst elements of Swinburne's nature and greatly accelerated his moral deterioration. In fact, Houghton became connected with de Sade in Swinburne's imagination—an association which suggests that more than a few similarities existed between de Sade's writings and Lord Houghton's private letters and conversation. In his letters to Houghton, Swinburne often addresses him as "mon cher Rodin." Rodin was the master of the pension of San Marcel, a house of the most questionable purposes and practices, in de Sade's writings.[28] Houghton obviously shared Swinburne's interest in flagellation, for in the same letter Swinburne says he is anxious to see the style of Houghton's flagellant fiction. This remark is in relation to chapters of a fictional work dealing with a schoolmaster's autobiography which both he and Houghton were apparently writing. In another letter to Houghton on February 3, 1863, Swinburne describes with ecstatic delight the proper way to flog a boy so as to raise red welts on his bottom,[29] and a week later he discusses the exquisite pleasure of being flogged in a room readied beforehand with burnt scents or in a grove of trees smelling of spring.[30]

These letters show clearly the damage done to Swinburne by his association with Houghton; they also prove beyond a reasonable doubt that Houghton had ominous traits in his own character that should be inquired into by his future biographers.

As in the case of Rossetti, Houghton's deleterious influence was increased by some of the people Swinburne met through him; but, because Houghton moved on a much higher social plane, their number was not so large nor their collective damage so serious as that done by the raffish hangers-on of the Pre-Raphaelites. The most outstanding of Houghton's acquaintances was Sir Richard Francis Burton (1821-1890), whom Swinburne met at one of Houghton's breakfasts on June 5, 1861.[31] Sixteen years older than Swinburne, a virile adventurer who had poked about the world in out-of-the-way places, Burton was perhaps overly fond of bawdry and alcohol, and he had a distinctly bad influence on Swinburne. The elder man encouraged Swinburne to the excessive drinking which soon became a major problem for him. Moreover, he introduced Swinburne into the sinister Cannibal Club, founded by Burton—whose travels had half convinced him of the benefits of anthropophagy—as an offshoot of the Anthropological Society.[32] For the club, which held its dinners under the symbol of a savage gnawing a human bone, Swinburne wrote the *Cannibal Catechism*, a parody of Christian prayer and religious teaching.[33]

Houghton's love of pornography led him to encourage Swinburne to write many of the most objectionable poems which later appeared in *Poems and Ballads* in 1866. Houghton then went about London spreading the word of the character of these poems. Houghton took a keen delight in bringing together at his home people of opposite tastes and ideas and setting them on each other. Swinburne and his poetry were surefire shockers for any but the most coarse Victorians, and Houghton made full use

of his young protégé. At Fryston in the summer of 1861 he had
him read his poems "The Leper" and "Les Noyades" before James
Spedding, then Archbishop of York, and Thackeray and his
daughters, who were in their early twenties.[34] Also at Fryston in
November, 1862—this time with no women present—he paraded
Swinburne before a company which included Lawrence Oliphant,
the novelist, and Henry Adams, the quiet and intelligent young
American serving as his father's secretary at the American Em-
bassy and perhaps meant by Houghton to be Swinburne's foil on
this occasion. In his *The Education of Henry Adams,* Adams gives
a notable description of the occasion and of Swinburne:

The fourth was a boy, or had the look of one, though in fact a year
older than Adams himself. He resembled in action . . . a tropical
bird, high-crested, long-beaked, quick-moving, with rapid utterance
and screams of humor, quite unlike any English lark or nightingale.
One could hardly call him a crimson macaw among owls, and yet no
ordinary contrast availed. Milnes introduced him as Mr. Algernon
Swinburne.[35]

After telling how, at a signal from Milnes, Swinburne broke
into a discourse lasting through the rest of the evening and far
surpassing any conversation Adams had ever heard, the American
describes with awe Swinburne's mental powers and the recitation
of his poems "Faustine," "Four Boards of the Coffin Lid," and the
"Ballad of Burdens," noting with curiosity that Milnes was "his
most appreciative" listener.

Houghton's crowning exhibition of his "tropical bird" came at
the Annual Dinner of the Royal Literary Fund on May 2, 1866.
As chairman of this affair, Houghton asked Swinburne to be on
the program. Swinburne, who very much disliked speaking before large groups, reluctantly consented and replied to the toast
for the imaginative literature of England by reading in a shrill
voice an essay on the reciprocal influence of English and French
literatures. He paid special tribute to his old idol Hugo, and he
gave considerable attention to Baudelaire and Arnold. This was
a worse breach of conduct than reading his poems of morbid love
to the Thackerays and to the Archbishop of York. For the guests
at the dinner were strongly Tory and strongly patriotic, toasting
the queen, the royal family, the Church, the Army and Navy, and

finally the Royal Literary Fund itself—all preceding the toast to the historical and imaginative literature of England. To inject any praise of French literature into such an affair was hardly in good taste, but to extol such a rabid iconoclast as Hugo and such a morbid pornographer as Baudelaire was an abomination. In its account of the affair *The Times* gave the substance of the various responses to the toasts at length, but of Swinburne it said merely, "Mr. Swinburne having also acknowledged the toast, Sir R. Murchison proposed 'Classical and Scientific Education.' " [36]

Precisely what Swinburne said has to this day never been printed in full, though Gosse gives an excerpt from it in his biography. The speech remains locked up in the archives of the Royal Literary Fund. The report of *The Times* is the fullest contemporary account we have of the dinner. There, like Alice in Wonderland after she had drunk from the little bottle, Swinburne and his ill-fated speech are shrunk to an absolute phrase of seven words.

Houghton's apparent inducement to win Swinburne's consent to speak before the Annual Dinner was the consideration that his appearance would introduce him to an important and influential segment of the literary "quality" of England and would thus prepare for a strong reception of *Poems and Ballads,* to appear in a few months. But in April, 1866, Swinburne wrote Houghton a brief note mentioning his intention of praising Hugo, Arnold, and Baudelaire. Houghton, well acquainted with the atmosphere and purpose of the dinners, must have known that any mention of Baudelaire and Hugo would be as out of place as a guffaw at a funeral. Yet he did nothing to save the situation. Our conclusion must be that this was one more instance of his damnable practice of throwing opposites together in order to witness their embarrassment. Exposing Swinburne to the cold contempt of the Annual Dinner was even more cruel than Rossetti's having him pose through a long morning kissing Fanny Cornforth. It was also much more costly. The way was prepared for a strong reception of *Poems and Ballads,* right enough; but the reception was with critical brickbats.

Following the debacle that attended the publication of *Poems and Ballads* in 1866, Swinburne soon learned that Houghton was a fair-weather friend whose affection warmed or cooled with the rise or fall of Swinburne's popularity. From that time he had little love for Houghton, whom he and Burton referred to derisively as "the Thermometer," though to Houghton's face he remained formally civil. And after July, 1872, when Rossetti cut Swinburne's acquaintance completely, his bitterness toward the artist increased as, with the passing years, he realized how he had been duped and made game of. In a letter to Watts-Dunton in 1877, he joined Rossetti and Houghton together as being both unmanly and immoral.[37] When Rossetti died in 1882, Swinburne came forth with a formal poetic tribute in "A Death on Easter Day," probably more because of his friendship with William Michael Rossetti than for any other reason. When Lord Houghton died at Vichy on August 11, 1885, Swinburne was silent.

· III   *The Rejected Lover*

One final cause of the downgrade course of Swinburne's life from 1860-1866 was his frustration in his love affair with Mary Gordon, which we have already mentioned. We have no means of knowing precisely when this love affair may have begun, but we are reasonably certain that it came to a climax in 1863-1864. After the death of his favorite sister Edith on September 23, 1863, Swinburne went to "Northcourt," Mary Gordon's home, and stayed there till February, 1864. During this period he worked hard on *Atalanta in Calydon* while Mary played Handel's music on the organ. For recreation they rode about the country; in between times, he helped her with a story she was writing, *The Children of the Chapel.*

At some time before, during, or after this visit, she told him she was going to marry Colonel Leith. In "The Triumph of Time" Swinburne sings the sad song of this affair, though of course without mentioning names or giving telltale clews as to who his beloved was. Until Professor Lang's article of 1959, Swinburnians always followed the lead of the Gosse biography of 1917 and believed that the girl was "Boo" Faulkner, who, as Lang shows, was only a child in 1863.[38] Mary Gordon, on the other hand, was only three years younger than Swinburne, and in 1863 he was twenty-six and she twenty-two or twenty-three. Under the circumstances, it is entirely possible that a love affair between them could have come to a climax in 1863, especially in a family where cousinly marriages were frequent.

On the strength of what Swinburne says in "The Triumph" and of what Mrs. Disney Leith (Mary Gordon) says in the preface to her biography of Swinburne, Professor Lang argues that Swinburne did not reveal his passion to her and that she, therefore, did not suspect it. Here I am skeptical for two reasons. First, Dickens and the other Romantic novelists to the contrary, women have an extrasensory apparatus that tells them when a man loves them, and I doubt that Mary Gordon, after the long years of close association with Swinburne, was an exception. Second, if Swinburne had admitted that he had proposed and that she had rejected him, it would have been an extremely humiliating admission for one with his physical handicap to make, and it would have necessitated an explanation as to why she turned him down —an explanation he and she very probably did not wish to give, or perhaps even to think about.

My guess (and in a case like this, one has to guess) is that Swinburne proposed and Mary Gordon turned him down because information about his debility had spread through the family; and her father, mother, and perhaps she herself, all agreed that there was no other course. In all likelihood they blamed his misfortune on too much inbreeding. To have had more of the same would have been to court even worse disaster. So she sadly said no; and, rather than explain why, she makes the flat denial in her preface.

There is no problem as to why he proposed. Nature does not wish abnormality, and even the most sexually abnormal person will from time to time experience impulses toward normalcy. But if such impulses only result in frustration, the victim retreats further into abnormality. And Swinburne's subsequent life followed this pattern. After returning to London, he rapidly completed *Atalanta* and then plunged into *Chastelard, Poems and Ballads,* and *Lesbia Brandon.* In his personal life he turned more and more to such sinister figures as Howell, Solomon, and Thomson. His letters through 1864 and 1865 show that his alcoholism had increased as had his tendency to revel in abnormal sexuality. The letters depict also a much greater absorption in the writings of de Sade. "The poet, thinker, and man of the world from whom the theology of my poem [*Atalanta*] is derived was a greater than Byron," he writes to Houghton in July, 1865. "*He* indeed, fatalist or not, saw to the bottom of gods and men." [39] And what de Sade saw at the "bottom," the statement implies, was lies and hypocrisy.

[77]

When success finally came with the publication of *Atalanta* in November, 1865, Swinburne grew worse instead of better. On about November 25, 1865, Scott wrote Lady Trevelyan from London that " . . . he suffers under a dislike to ladies of late—his knowledge of himself and of them increasing upon him." [40] In *Chastelard,* soon to be published, Scott advised her, she would find evidence of this "insaneness of the impulses" which had now so excited Swinburne and driven him so to alcohol that both Dante Gabriel and William Rossetti felt he could not live long if he continued.

Alcoholism soon betrayed him into public disgrace. On December 13, 1865, he infuriated Lord Houghton by being late for an evening gathering where Houghton introduced him to Tennyson.[41] After the introduction, Swinburne turned his back on Tennyson and went into another room where he talked so loudly with Palgrave and George Lewes that he disturbed Tennyson and the rest of the gathering. Later, Houghton upbraided him and accused him of being drunk, as he probably was. At the Arts Club in February, 1866, Swinburne shocked the members by his "fearful language" and came near to being expelled.[42] In her last illness at Neuchatel in May, Lady Trevelyan asked Ruskin anxiously what he thought would be the final outcome of Swinburne's mad conduct; the only reassurance he could give her was that God had given him so much genius He would not let him perish —that Swinburne's good side would eventually triumph.[43]

But in December, 1866, things had come to such a pass that Swinburne was recuperating at "Holmwood," where the Admiral had moved his family from the Isle of Wight in 1865.[44] Thereafter the story was often repeated of the old Admiral's coming to take his son home to nurse him back to health and strength until the old man's death in 1877. From 1877 to 1879 there was nobody to perform this office until Walter Theodore Watts carried Swinburne from his rooms in an almost dying condition to the solitude of Putney in July, 1879. Gradually and persistently, Watts ruled out of Swinburne's life, one by one, the various parasites and noxious influences which had clustered about him since he first came to London. It was high time somebody did him this service; otherwise his death would have surely been an event of 1879 or 1880.

IV *Swinburne the Artist*

In addition to the harm done his character and reputation through his association with Houghton and Rossetti, Swinburne's artistic development suffered even more seriously. These were the years when he should have been finding himself and his proper place in the world and in the literary firmament. These were the years when he should have been learning to know himself; when he should have developed his personal philosophy of life; when he should have gauged his literary genius, its range, its capabilities, its limitations. These were the years when he should have pondered the world about him and fitted it and himself into the great sweep of history. This was surely the period when the artist in him should have burgeoned into strength and accomplishment.

For it is a truism that no artist can rise to the full height of his powers until his feet rest on the bedrock of a settled philosophy and until he feels confident of himself and of what he is doing. He must likewise find his own answers to the great questions of life. But Swinburne's vassalage to Rossetti and Houghton did much to prevent him from developing a personal philosophy or from engaging in a trial-and-error search for his own answers. Instead, he took their philosophies and their answers and labored unsuccessfully to distort his own individuality so as to conform to them. In 1861 George Meredith put his finger squarely on Swinburne's major weakness when he wrote of him: ". . . I don't see any internal centre from which springs anything that he does. He will make a great name, but whether he is to distinguish himself solidly as an Artist, I would not willingly prognosticate." [45]

To the end of his life, Swinburne never succeeded in achieving the "internal centre," or hard core of individuality, without which he could not achieve the greatness of Browning, Tennyson, or Arnold. Perhaps his physical handicap would have rendered such development impossible for him even had he not been dominated by Rossetti and Houghton, but we can safely say that he would have attained his mental, moral, and artistic maturity more satisfactorily and completely without their noisome influence.

CHAPTER 5

Literature for Art's Sake

NOTHING furnishes a better illustration of the reflective quality of Swinburne's writings than a comparison of the works
produced from 1860 to 1866 with the course of his life and
thought during those years. The hallmark of the Romanticist is
his absorption in himself and his reactions to life—his experiences, his longings, his loves, his triumphs, his frustrations, his
hatreds—and so it was with Swinburne. As he lived, he wrote.
We can clearly discern the devotion to Pre-Raphaelitism, the increasing boldness with which he followed and practiced the tenets of French aestheticism, the consequent flaunting of the algolagnia in his nature, the passionate hope and longing of the love
affair, and the bitter self-pity when he experienced defeat. We
can discern also the progressive deterioration of his character, in-
terrupted for a few months during which he rose to the lyric ecstasy of love, but resumed and hastened after his rejection.

Apparently, as the man deteriorated, the writing power grew.
This phenomenon has led to the popular claim not only that,
somehow, his genius required the fuel of dissipation to bring it
to its brightest flame, but that when the tedious Watts-Dunton
took charge and eliminated the dissipation, the flame subsided
and, but for an occasional fitful glow, went out. This view I cannot accept. I believe the rise of his genius took place despite the
dissipations, not because of them. Swinburne, after all, was at
the time of life when artistic genius usually rises rapidly if the
conditions of the poet's environment stir and excite him. And
Swinburne, free of the restraints of home and Oxford, was greatly
exhilarated by the impact of London and the brilliant minds he
encountered there. Furthermore, he was profoundly moved by
grief over the loss of his favorite sister Edith in the fall of 1863,
and by his passion for Mary Gordon, which rose to a climax dur-

ing his three months' stay at her home after Edith's death. These two events combined to rouse him from the opium dream that his life in London had become and to lift his genius to the heights of *Atalanta in Calydon* and to the best pieces of *Poems and Ballads*. The bitter hopelessness that took hold after he left Mary Gordon plunged him once more into the depths of algolagnia and led to that epic of abnormality, *Chastelard,* and to the worst poems of *Poems and Ballads*.

I The Queen Mother *and* Rosamond

Written during his last year at Oxford and published toward the end of 1860, the play *The Queen Mother* strongly resembles Swinburne's earlier Elizabethan imitations. Queen Catherine di Medici, mother of King Charles IX of France, sets her maid of honor Denise to persuade the king to order the St. Bartholomew Massacre. Queen Catherine knows that the king is in love with Denise, but does not suspect Denise's complete opposition to the bloody scheme. When the Queen learns that Denise has instead tried to dissuade Charles from the atrocity, she has her imprisoned on the charge of poisoning the jester Cino.

The play reaches its climax in the Massacre, which Swinburne depicts with many bloody scenes. During the carnage, King Charles himself wounds a girl with his harquebus and then is grief-stricken when he discovers that it is his beloved Denise. The play ends with the perfidious Queen Mother completely successful in her diabolical schemes, yet she confesses that she feels a twinge of pity for Denise, now dead of her wound.

The chief fault with this play is that there is no central theme. Catherine is obviously meant to be the most important character as well as the mainspring that keeps the plot in motion. But Swinburne gives her no fundamental philosophy to account for her deviltry; she is not fanatically religious nor is she motivated by a profound hatred of the Huguenots, who have done her no harm. She desires and brings about the deaths of thousands of innocent people for no more comprehensible reason than that she is a villainess and must, therefore, engage in villainy. King Charles is a portrait only partially finished. Sadistic and admitted even by his own mother to be a weak fool, he shows pathos and nobility in his grief over the death of Denise. Perhaps the best character creation is the jester Cino, who parries and thrusts with such brilliant wit that we could wish Swinburne had devoted himself to comedy rather than tragedy.

He would have done a better play had he not been still laboring under the Elizabethan complex. Marlowe's mighty line in the heavy accents of blank verse style, with a labored attempt by Swinburne to imitate Elizabethan diction, only loads the play down with much verbiage. Had he written the play in prose and in the language of his own day, he might have had a stage success. But even with all its faults, it tells an intricate and interesting story well and carries the reader with it till the end.

Rosamond, also an Oxford product, was written and rewritten several times before it reached its final form. Based upon a twelfth-century legend about Henry II and Rosamond Clifford, reputedly the King's mistress, this is a dramatic poem rather than a drama. Because Rosamond was said to be buried in a convent near Oxford, Swinburne's interest in her may have come from his readings in the library and his walks through the countryside.

As Swinburne tells the story, a Pre-Raphaelite picture comes to life. Briefly, the plot centers around the love of King Henry II for Rosamond, with the third angle of the triangle formed by Queen Eleanor, whose jealousy and hatred drive her to seek revenge by poisoning her rival. Rosamond is the melancholy Pre-Raphaelite beauty of medieval times who is so carried away by a sensuous passion for the King that she is willing to sacrifice both her honor and her life for it.

Unlike *The Queen Mother, Rosamond* has a theme of "all for love," which is adhered to with some consistency. In all other respects, however, it falls far short of the other work, and its greatest fault is its lack of clarity. Because Swinburne assumes that his readers are familiar with the story, he omits such important details as Rosamond's labyrinthine bower and the use of the silk cord by the queen and her accomplice to penetrate the maze. Also in the first scene of the poem-play, Rosamond's companion Constance soliloquizes about her intention of betraying Rosamond; but, as we never see her again, we don't know whether she does or not. In several other passages the meaning is unclear. Most of this obscurity comes from Swinburne's deliberate imitation of Browning's style and technique in *Pippa Passes.* He succeeds so well that his story is even more of a puzzle than Browning's.

The distorted side of Swinburne's nature is evident in several references to flagellation: in the King's and Rosamond's confession that their love is composed of pain and pleasure; and in the extreme sadism with which the Queen torments Rosamond, seizing her by the hair and pinching her throat, before she finally forces her to drink the poison.

We may with justice consider *The Queen Mother* the first of Swinburne's adult works, but its many inadequacies place *Rosamond* as the last of the juvenilia.

II *Pieces for Periodicals*

Swinburne's five articles about Hugo's *Les Miserables* were published in the *Spectator* from April to September, 1862. He wrote each article as each part of the book was published, admittedly a poor way of criticizing a book. All the articles are highly laudatory, with here and there a slight objection or difference of opinion with Hugo. In the second article Swinburne makes it quite clear that his critical criteria rest squarely on the dogmas of *Ars Gratia Artis:* "Any book above a certain pitch of writing must be taken first of all to be a work of pure art. For we can bring no man's work to a higher standard. All the excellence of moral purpose in the world will never serve for salt to a thing born rotten." [1]

We can discern a clash within Swinburne between his great admiration for Hugo on literary and republican grounds on the one hand and his devotion to "art for art's sake" on the other. Though he couples Hugo's name with Shakespeare's and hails him as "the greatest master we have alive" and as "the one supremely great modern dramatist," he is clearly disturbed by Hugo's underlying moral purpose in *Les Miserables,* which is to drive home to his readers his conviction that all social ills can be cured by light and reason. Undoubtedly, Swinburne had Baudelaire's doctrine of the beauty of evil in mind when he wrote: "Besides, if the thing were possible, would it be a thing to wish for? To live in a world with the evil drained off would be a heavy and hopeless kind of life." [2]

Interesting to note are Swinburne's references to fictitious French poets and critics, Félicien Cossu and Ernest Clouet, in the articles in the *Spectator* for July 26 and August 16, 1862. Apparently, he was thus early preparing Editor Hutton for the hoaxes he hoped to put over on him in the following December. In both articles he quotes these two, deprecating their lavish styles but admitting some truth in what they say.

In December he sent in pretended reviews of Félicien Cossu's *Les Amours Étiques* and Clouet's *Les Abîmes,* both books as fictitious as the authors. *Les Amours Étiques* was purportedly a book of poems with such provocative titles as "The Sigh" ("At fifteen years I am no more a virgin"), "The Broken Wing," "A Night of Sodom," "Poor Girl," "Spasm of Love," and "Rictus." [3] Clouet's *Les Abîmes* Swinburne attempted to pass off as a book of essays on such matters as the relations of Joan of Arc with Gilles de Rais, an account of the *Fragoletta* of Latouche, and a lengthy eulogy of the Marquis de Sade.[4]

Swinburne's method was to quote lengthily from these two works, expressing his disapproval as he did so—a good dodge for getting them printed for the British public and the same scheme he had used in his review of Baudelaire. This time it did not work, though it came close. The article on Clouet was in galley proof before Hutton wrote Swinburne that the subject was obscene and that his tone was not so condemnatory as it should have been.[5]

Precisely what was Swinburne's object in this matter? Either he resented the strictures against French literature made by British critics and wished to pull their legs, or the article on Baudelaire had brought protests from so many subscribers that Hutton had expressed his displeasure to Swinburne, who took this method of getting even. Hutton and Swinburne were poles apart in their views on morality. In a note appended to Swinburne's letter to the editor of the *Spectator* defending Meredith's *Modern Love,* Hutton stated that he had written the original review which called forth Swinburne's disapproval.[6] In the review, Hutton had objected to the "wretched jocularity" of tone of some of the *Modern Love* sonnets and suggested that a better title would have been "Modern Lust." If Swinburne could have gotten one or both of his articles past Hutton, it would have made the editor look foolish because in a short time someone would have discovered that no such men or books existed.

It is highly possible that Hutton did not discover the hoax, but that some friend did and warned him in time to prevent the catastrophe. After all, an editor is duty bound to read and pass on copy before it gets into galley proof. He would hardly have neglected to do so with the contributions of such an erratic personality as Swinburne. Presumably, then, he had read and approved the article; and, had he not been warned, it would have appeared in the *Spectator*.

The evidence points to Lord Houghton as the friend in the case. In a letter on August 18, 1862, Swinburne asks Houghton if he can locate the missing last leaf of his article on Cossu, and elsewhere in this letter refers to "our common friend M. F. Cossu," indicating his sharing the joke with Houghton.[7] Houghton's warning to Hutton would be an obligation because it was through Houghton that Hutton had met Swinburne and accepted his work. The warning was probably accompanied by Houghton's request that Hutton not indicate to Swinburne his awareness of the burlesque but reject it as immoral. Otherwise Swinburne would have surely suspected Houghton, and Houghton was having too much fun with this odd genius to wish to lose him just yet.

Swinburne's practical joke was of course nothing short of journalistic treachery and an inexcusable betrayal of trust. Even had he succeeded, subsequent certain exposure would have ended his career with the *Spectator*. As it turned out, his career ended and a lifelong enmity sprang up between him and his former editor.

III   Atalanta in Calydon

Although critics disagree about many things concerning Swinburne, they are almost unanimous in acclaiming *Atalanta in Calydon* to be one of the greatest of his works. Constructed on the rather obscure Greek legend recounted by Ovid in the *Metamorphoses*, and with the theme of man's helplessness to avoid an inexorable fate, this poem has a scope and magnificence absent in most of Swinburne's works.

What led him to return to the classical material, when since 1857 his attention had been focused on Pre-Raphaelite medievalism and, at least since 1859, on French aestheticism? When the poem was taking shape in his mind, from August, 1863, to February, 1864, he was away from London and Rossetti, first at "East Dene" and later with Mary Gordon at "Northcourt." Had his disillusionment with Rossetti that came when Fanny Cornforth moved into Tudor House brought a corresponding disillusionment with Pre-Raphaelitism, and did he turn to classicism for relief? Or was it that in this poem he wished to deal with matters concerning his relationship to his family and felt that the classical framework would provide a more noble vehicle as well as a more effective disguise?

Whatever the cause, Swinburne selected a pre-Trojan War Greek myth of a minor nature and clothed it with inspired verse. When Meleager, the son of King Oeneus of Calydon and of Queen Althaea, is born the three Fates are present. Clotho prophesies that he will have courage; Lachesis, that he will have strength; and Atropos, that his life will last only until the brand then on the fire is burnt to ashes. Althaea promptly seizes the brand, puts out the fire, and hides the charred remains in a safe place.

When Meleager approaches manhood, Oeneus sacrifices to the gods; but, through an oversight, he neglects to include Artemis, goddess of the hunt. After the fashion of slighted goddesses, Artemis takes her revenge by sending a huge boar to lay waste the vineyards, olive groves, and farmland of Calydon and to fill its people with terror. Meleager, determined to end this nuisance, invites heroes from all of Greece to join him in the hunt. Among those who respond are Castor, Pollux, Nestor, Theseus, Pirithous, Peleus, Jason, Admetus, and Anceus. Noteworthy among them is Atalanta of Arcadia, cared for by a bear in childhood, and now an able huntress and a beautiful girl. Meleager falls in love with her almost immediately, but his two uncles, Toxeus and Plexippus, Queen Althaea's brothers and also in the hunting party, are highly offended at the intrusion of an Arcadian girl into the masculine sport, and make such insulting remarks about her that Meleager can hold his temper only with difficulty.

After the usual banquets and merrymaking, the hunt begins. Hearing their calls, the boar rushes forth from the swamp and attacks them. Jason's spear only grazes him. Atalanta coolly shoots an arrow and wounds him, but not seriously. Anceus is a casualty to the boar's fierce tusk before Meleager ends the fight and kills the boar by plunging his spear into the beast and giving it successive deadly blows.

The shouts of the others acclaiming his triumph die into envious murmurs when Meleager awards the boar's head and skin to Atalanta. Especially angry are the jealous uncles Toxeus and

Plexippus, who interpret the giving of the trophies to the foreign Atalanta as an insult to their masculinity and to their country. Now they rush forward to snatch the trophies, vowing that no Arcadian will have these as grounds for taunts in the future. Enraged, Meleager slays them on the spot.

Ironically, the news of the tragedy comes to Althaea as she is making an offering of thanks in the temple for the slaying of the boar. Her grief for her beloved brothers turns into such anger at Meleager that she takes out the fateful brand, throws it into the fire, and watches it burn. Shortly afterward, another messenger enters with the tragic news that Meleager, unaccountably and mysteriously stricken as he and his triumphant party were making their way home, is dying.

Here Swinburne violates the Greek dramatic unity of place by shifting to the site where Meleager lies, surrounded by King Oeneus, Atalanta, and the others of the hunting party. Intuitively, Meleager knows that his mother has caused his death, but he forgives her because she, like himself, has only been the pawn of fate. Begging his kinsmen to remember his good deeds, he expires as the chorus solemnly intones the reflection that man cannot overcome the immortal gods.

As Swinburne tells the story, it has several points of difference from the version given by Ovid in the *Metamorphoses*, probably Swinburne's main source. Ovid tells it as an incident; Swinburne blows it up almost to epic proportions, nearly ten times the length of Ovid's tale. Ovid also makes light of the love strain. In Ovid's version before the hunt begins, Meleager feels a passion for Atalanta, but he resolutely suppresses it and centers his attention on the hunt. Swinburne makes the love factor the mainspring of the story—Althaea senses impending doom in her son's attraction to Atalanta, whom she finds unwomanly, and warns him against her; but he reminds her that he is a man grown, has proven his courage with Jason and the Argonauts, and has never seen a woman as "fair and fearful" as Atalanta.

Swinburne likewise has King Oeneus adding his voice to Althaea's, pointing out that Atalanta is designed by the gods for celibacy and is not the kind of girl who makes a good wife. Althaea begs her son not to bring about her death by perversely "following strange loves," but Meleager answers that he must live out his life as Zeus has planned it and regardless of the consequences. The chorus breaks in with a song prophetic of love attended by fate and death.

Before the hunt begins, in the ugly scene that takes place between Meleager and his uncles Plexippus and Toxeus, who sneer that his speech in praise of Atalanta is "woman-tongued" and will not slay any boars, Atalanta defends herself as living the life chosen for her by the gods, a life of unwed loneliness and childlessness; she promises that, when the hunt is over, she will leave Calydon forever.

None of this material is included in the *Metamorphoses*, but in Swinburne's version it darkens the sky and prepares the way for the tragic denouement. Here again are marked differences between the two stories. Ovid shows Meleager dying quickly and apparently without suspicion that Althaea has been the agent of his calamity, but Swinburne portrays Meleager as fully cognizant that his death is the result of his mother's wish and act. As soon as the messenger reports to Althaea that he has been stricken, the scene shifts again to the members of the hunting party as they stand about the expiring hero. There follows a climactic scene much like the finale of an opera, with the leading actors present —except Althaea—and each sings his own lines to his own music, but all blend into a harmonious whole with the chorus in the background. Atalanta regrets that she came to Calydon, Meleager consoles her by blaming the tragedy on fate, King Oeneus is grief-stricken at the loss of such a son, and the chorus intones a chant of the awful power of the gods. The trio and the chorus are succeeded by a long solo speech by Meleager in which he forgives his absent mother as the instrument of fate and calls upon her and his friends not to let his memory die among men. Then, turning to Atalanta, he asks her to kiss him, to mourn for him, and to let no man say his death was "woman-wise" and "dishonourable."

It is easy to read all kinds of autobiographical significance into *Atalanta* and undoubtedly much of it is genuinely there. The somber tone and the pervasive tragic gloom came from the painful loss of a beloved sister. Edith's death was the first break in Swinburne's immediate family circle; it placed him face to face with eternity and forced him to reexamine the course of his own life and his own negative philosophy. It gave him an epic view of himself in relation to the world about him which he had not had before and which may have been the result of his mother's pleadings at this time. For the rest of her life, his mother hoped and prayed that he would return to the religious belief of his youth. What could have been more natural than for her to have used these hours of grief to point out to him the folly of the life he had been living in London and its inevitable consequences?

If we accept Professor Lang's theory that Swinburne's love for Mary Gordon mounted to a climax and resulted in frustrating emotional defeat in the months following Edith's death, Swinburne's emphasis upon the love of Meleager for Atalanta is understandable on autobiographical grounds. Of course, Swinburne's concept of the story as a tragedy growing out of Artemis' desire for revenge and of her use of the boar and Atalanta as instruments of attaining that revenge necessitates the emphasis upon the love theme and its fatal aspects. But it neither necessitates nor explains the lyrical joy of the opening chorus, "When the hounds of the spring are on winter's traces," nor the closing scene of self-pity in which Meleager makes his final request of Atalanta:

> *But thou, dear, hide my body with thy veil,*
> *And with thy raiment cover foot and head,*
> *And stretch thyself upon me and touch hands*
> *With hands and lips with lips: be pitiful*
> *As thou art maiden perfect; let no man*
> *Defile me to despise me, saying, This man*
> *Died woman-wise, a woman's offering, slain*
> *Through female fingers in his woof of life,*
> *Dishonourable. . . .*[8]

The initial joy is too joyful for the purposes of Greek tragedy—but not for a young poet experiencing for the first time the delirium of love. The closing self-pity and the request for the girl to stretch her body upon his in a last embrace will hardly do for a Greek hero, but it would not be out of character for such a person as Swinburne—hurt, depressed, full of self-pity after his rejection by Mary Gordon—to have given release to his feelings in such a dream.

In this connection also, Swinburne's description of Atalanta as fearless, athletic, and beautiful in an almost masculine fashion is not out of keeping with a description of Mary Gordon, who loved to ride horseback with him and who is reported to have swum at seventy in the Arctic Ocean.[9] Notable, too, is the fact that after Swinburne's death, Mrs. Mary Gordon Leith did her utmost to carry out Meleager's request to Atalanta to "let no man defile me to despise me" by fiercely denying anything in any way derogatory to his reputation[10] and by publishing her memoir in conjunction with the carefully censored family letters to give substance to the image of him she wished the world to have.

Meleager's wish for Atalanta to lay herself upon him and to embrace him is only one of several bits of evidence about Swinburne's abnormality. Others include Althaea's warning Meleager that his "following strange loves" will "kill mine heart," [11] Meleager's description of Atalanta's masculine beauty with her "hallowed hair" and swift feet,[12] Plexippus' taunts that Meleager is effeminate ("a man grown girl").[13] The chorus's sadic description of the malignant gods who have created man only that they might take pleasure in his anguish is also in this direction.

> Who gives a star and takes a sun away;
> Who shapes the soul, and makes her a barren wife
>   To the earthly body and grievous growth of clay;
> Who turns the large limbs to a little flame
>   And binds the great sea with a little sand;
> Who makes desire, and slays desire with shame;
>   Who shakes the heaven as ashes in his hand;
> Who, seeing the light and shadow for the same,
>   Bids day waste night as fire devours a brand,
> Smites without sword, and scourges without rod;
>   The supreme evil, God.
> Yea, with thine hate, O God, thou hast covered us. . . .[14]

Can we doubt that this was Swinburne's passionate protest for his bereavement, perhaps for his frustrated love, and certainly for the malformation of his physical and mental being?

All such biographical factors are of prime interest to the biographer; our main concern is with the work. *Atalanta* is truly a great achievement. The theme of fate is superbly enunciated and executed with all the pieces blending into a splendid mosaic. Swinburne has turned Ovid's incident into an authentic and magnificent tragedy with a universal significance. Meleager is any man caught in the grip of forces he cannot withstand; Althaea is the tragic mother, filled with foreboding, who sees her child, heedless of her warnings, headed toward inevitable disaster. The weak link in the chain of events is her unmotherly act of sentencing her son to death for his defensible slaying of the two carping uncles, but this detail Swinburne inherited from mythology and probably felt he dared not change. Swinburne's title is also poorly chosen: the tragedy is Althaea's, not Atalanta's, and the title is therefore misleading. Although she is the root of the tragedy, Atalanta stands by as a spectator, not at all returning Meleager's love, and responding to his final passionate speech only with the words that she is sad and must go home.

Despite these minor shortcomings, this is a truly great poem, fittingly hailed as the greatest English achievement in the classical vein and the nearest approach to classical mood and tone. In *Atalanta* Swinburne found his true voice. Most of the story is told in blank verse, with variant meters used in the songs; but the blank verse has a new surge and accent—it is no longer imitative of Elizabethan blank verse but truly Swinburnian. He himself was aware that he had found new power. In a letter to his sister Alice on December 31, 1863, Swinburne told of his delight in listening to Mary Gordon play Handel's music on the organ at "Northcourt" while he wrote *Atalanta:* "It crams and crowds me with old and new verses, half-remembered and half-made, which new ones will hardly come straight afterwards: but under their influence I have done some more of my Atalanta which will be among my great doings if it keeps up with its own last scenes throughout." [15]

Since the great Christmas music of Handel is his *Messiah,* a reasonable conjecture is that this was the music played. A musical epic whose theme is the birth of Christ and the Redemption of man, its music surges with triumph and jubilation. Many of its choral and solo tempos are in three-four, three-eight, six-eight, and twelve-eight time, musical equivalents of the dactyl and spondee, necessitated in the *Messiah* by a libretto which favors such meters. For instance, the opening chorus is, "And the glory of the Lord shall be revealed, and all flesh shall see it together"; the next, "And he shall purify the sons of Levi, that they may offer unto the Lord an offering in righteousness"; the next, "O thou that tellest good tidings to Zion, arise, say unto the cities of Judah, Behold your God!" and so on.

Swinburne's blank verse has the same epic quality, the same

organ roll, the same triumphant stride and exuberance. *Atalanta* opens with this prayer of the chief huntsman to Artemis:

> *Maiden, and mistress of the months and stars*
> *Now folded in the flowerless fields of heaven,*
> *Goddess whom all gods love with threefold heart,*
> *Being treble in thy divided deity,*
> *A light for dead men and dark hours, a foot*
> *Swift on the hills as morning, and a hand*
> *To all things fierce and fleet that roar and range*
> *Mortal, with gentler shafts than snow or sleep. . . .*[16]

He increases the anapests, shortens the line to tetrameter, and employs rhyme to give the effect of boundless joy in the greatest lyric he ever wrote, a lyric which equals the best of Shelley or Burns:

> *When the hounds of spring are on winter's traces,*
> *The mother of months in meadow or plain*
> *Fills the shadows and windy places*
> *With lisp of leaves and ripple of rain;*
> *And the brown bright nightingale amorous*
> *Is half assuaged for Itylus,*
> *For the Thracian ships and the foreign faces,*
> *The tongueless vigil, and all the pain.*[17]

As we said before, in *Atalanta* he stood on the threshold of a new world of great promise and achievement. But like Meleager, he saw his dreams vanish in the dark clouds of a bitter fate, and his hopes burnt to ashes like the fatal brand that ended his hero's life. With bitterness in his heart he descended once again and with greater desperation into the corrosive life of London.

IV Chastelard

Although Swinburne had begun *Chastelard* at Oxford and had completed it by the spring of 1863, he did not publish it until August, 1865.[18] The reason for the delay was that several of his friends—Ruskin, Meredith, possibly even Rossetti and Lord Houghton—to whom he had shown *Chastelard* and the poems he later gathered together into *Poems and Ballads* (1866), strongly advised against publication. Ruskin's opinion that they would give him a bad reputation was shared by the others.[19] Swinburne put *Chastelard* aside and wrote *Atalanta*.

The accolade that greeted *Atalanta* filled him with confidence that the time was ripe for a frontal assault on the ramparts of British Philistinism, or Utilitarianism—such an assault as had been made in France by Gautier and Baudelaire. Swinburne saw the Philistines as more than enemies of art; they also were his personal foes. They represented the forces of political Toryism and religious orthodoxy against which he had rebelled since his days at Eton. They were the conservatives who sat smugly by while the Austrians tyrannized Italy and while Louis Napoleon declared himself emperor of France. They were the blunt-spoken pragmatists who demanded of everything, art included, "What good is it? What can it be used for?" They were the snobs—at Eton, at Oxford, in his own family—who regarded Algernon Swinburne as an absurd oddity and listened to his tirades with amused derision. They represented the spirit which led Mary Gordon to reject him in favor of a "solid" man many years older. They were, in short, just about everyone and everything in Britain that Swinburne hated.

His warfare against the Philistines was nothing new. At least since his first year at Oxford he had berated the Philistine spirit in his verse, and several letters from 1860 to 1866 show his mounting scorn. Writing to William Bell Scott in 1865, he sneers at Browning as a "Philistine idol" and promises that " '. . . that twice-battered God of Palestine,' Dagon-Caliban, shall 'wear my stripes impressed on him, and bear my beating to his grave.' " [20] The letter defending Meredith's *Modern Love* sonnets and the articles on Hugo in the *Spectator* in 1862 had denied the validity of moral purpose in literature. The article on Baudelaire's *Les Fleurs du Mal* had, as we have seen, gone a step further with a bold acceptance of the beauty of evil. Now, the almost unanimous praise of *Atalanta* and the spirit of defiance that grew great through 1865 led him to abandon caution altogether.

His next step was probably suggested to him by *Les Fleurs du Mal*. Up to now he had been an English disciple of Baudelaire. But why remain a disciple? Why not become the English Baudelaire in very fact and perhaps even go beyond the master? Why not "poke up" the British Philistines with a whole series of "evil flowers" of his own—works in poetry and prose which would drag into the open the evil side of human nature and flaunt it before the hypocritical Philistines? Swinburne's *Les Fleurs du Mal* was to be five works in four different types of literature: the drama *Chastelard,* the *Poems and Ballads,* the novels *Love's Cross-Currents* and *Lesbia Brandon,* and the critical work about William Blake.

Chastelard made a good opening gun in the campaign. Its plot centers around the love of the French courtier Chastelard for Queen Mary of Scotland, whom he has followed from France to her native land. Two subplots—the affair between Darnley and Mary Hamilton, one of Queen Mary's maids-in-waiting, and that of the love of Mary Beaton, another of the queen's maids, for Chastelard—complicate the structure. After a love scene with Chastelard, the unpredictable queen announces her intention of marrying Darnley and of making him king of Scotland.

Chastelard secretes himself under the queen's bed on the night of her wedding to Darnley, and, when she is alone and undressing, he announces himself. At first very angry with the youth, the queen soon relents, confesses her love for him, and they embrace violently. He refuses her pleas to leave before Darnley comes; Darnley's arrival begins a tempestuous scene in which he accuses the queen of infidelity with Chastelard and in which Chastelard threatens to kill Darnley. The scene ends with Darnley partially convinced of the queen's innocence and with Chastelard arrested and imprisoned. Then follows a bewildering number of contradictions and vacillations on the part of the queen, who permits Chastelard's execution and who leans forward with evident joy as his head falls.

Told in five acts and employing blank verse, *Chastelard* has no discernible theme except for the strange love of a rather abnormal youth for a most abnormal woman. In the play Swinburne gave free reign to his passion for being hurt by a beautiful female: In one scene the queen tells Chastelard of her dream of dancing with him wearing a mask and his lips "sewn up close/ With scarlet thread all dabbled wet in blood." [21] And when Mary Beaton points out the probable consequences of his hiding under the queen's bed, he replies that to shed his blood for her would be an ideal death. All in all, *Chastelard* is a worthless work, filled, as William Bell Scott said, with "insaneness of the impulses." [22] We could wish that a great poet had found better employment for his time.

The reception of *Chastelard* proved the wisdom of Ruskin's original advice not to publish it. The *Spectator* took Swinburne to task for reveling in the bestial passions of lust and confessed that it laid *Chastelard* down "with a sense of profound thankfulness that we have at last got out of the oppressive atmosphere in that forcing-house of sensual appetite into the open air." [23] James Russell Lowell, in the *North American Review,* sneered that it was only "the school exercise of a young poet learning to write." [24] In the *Fortnightly* Lord Houghton admitted that the play showed "faults of sensuousness, even of coarseness," but insisted that these were counterbalanced by "exceeding tenderness and refined emotion." [25] At a gathering of noted men in London, Tennyson said his objections to it were "as deep as Heaven and Hell." [26]

Such comments did not constitute a nest of aroused hornets, but they were the rumblings of a threatening storm that a cautious man would have heeded. Instead, Swinburne set about the publication of *Poems and Ballads.*

V Byron

Following the success of *Atalanta,* Bertram Payne of Moxon's asked Swinburne to edit a book of selections from the poems of Byron for the series called *Moxon's Miniature Poets.* Swinburne did so, wrote a critical introductory essay, and *Byron* appeared in March, 1866. As in almost all Swinburne's critical writings, his appraisal of Byron contains a strong personal note. Certainly he was thinking of himself and of his rough handling by the reviewers of *Chastelard* when he wrote that Byron had three handicaps: "youth, and genius, and an ancient name," and that ". . . every hound and every hireling lavished upon him the loathsome tribune of their abuse; all nameless creatures that nibble and prowl, upon whom the serpent's curse has fallen, to go upon his belly and eat dust all the days of his life, assailed him with their foulest venom and their keenest fangs." [27]

Nevertheless, as criticism his essay on Byron is one of Swinburne's better efforts, for he strives to be impartial. He scores Byron's faulty sense of meter, his too great love of applause, the lack of grace and wit in the early satires; he finds him supreme in the later satires like *Don Juan* and "The Vision of Judgment." As a poet, he rates him below Wordsworth and Landor; but Swinburne finds Byron's treatment of his material superior to Wordsworth's. Wordsworth, he says, is guilty of misusing nature for didactic purposes.

Almost the only notice of the *Byron* was in the *Spectator,* which took issue with Swinburne for praising Byron and for condemning the Philistines who warred against him. Byron, said the *Spectator,* had brought down upon his own head the just wrath of the so-called Philistines; then it observed somewhat ominously that Swinburne appeared to desire a like fate.[28]

VI Poems and Ballads (*1866*)

"I went to see Swinburne yesterday and heard some of the wickedest and splendidest verses ever written by a human creature," wrote John Ruskin to Lady Trevelyan on December 8, 1865. "He drank three bottles of porter while I was there. I don't know what to do with him or for him, but he mustn't publish these things. He speaks with immense gratitude of you—please tell him he mustn't." [29] Ruskin didn't know it, but Lady Trevelyan had already written Swinburne on December 6, begging him to be cautious of what poems he included in *Poems and Ballads* and reminding him how near he had come to disaster in *Chastelard.* "Don't give people a handle against you now," she warned. "And do mind what you say for the sake of all to whom your fame is dear, and who are looking forward to your career with hope and interest. . . ." [30]

Her admonition to guard his talk is in reference to a letter she wrote him on or about December 1, 1865, a letter which we do not have but the content of which we can easily deduce from his answering letters to her on December 4 and 5. Her missing letter warned him against publicly expressing his approval of the ancient Greek practice of pederasty, with either a direct statement or a strong implication that he had proclaimed his own participation in such a practice and saw nothing wrong with it. His letters to her are violent denials of such charges—too violent to be completely convincing—coupled with almost tearful gratitude for her friendship and kindness.[31]

But by December 10 he had regained his composure. His letter to her of that date is aloof. He has written nothing to be ashamed of, he tells her. No two of his friends agree on their criticism of his poems; almost everything he has written he has been advised by somebody or other to suppress. Ruskin, when he heard the poems, seemed to enjoy and accept them—could there be a fairer judge? If all Swinburne's friends disapproved of any poem, it would be omitted; otherwise, he implies, he will have to learn to live with the conviction that anything he writes will displease somebody. He will therefore follow his own judgment.[32]

Poems and Ballads should have come out in May, 1866, but the printers' errors and other delays of one sort or another deferred it till the end of July. The die was irrevocably cast, and in short order Swinburne was to learn the wisdom of Lady Trevelyan's disregarded advice.

Sixty-two poems make up the historic book. They range from verses he had composed at Oxford in 1858-1859 to some written as late as 1865 or early 1866; in length they vary from "Dolores" of fifty-five stanzas and 440 lines to the "Rondel" of twelve lines. The classification of content is somewhat complex and involved, as might be expected in a catchall volume of verse. Two of them, "A Song in Time of Order. 1852" and "A Song in Time of Revolution. 1860," express his republican hatred of Napoleon III, the Pope, and the Emperor of Austria, as well as his hope that they would be overthrown and liberty won through revolution. "In Memory of Walter Savage Landor," "To Victor Hugo," and "Dedication" ("To my friend, Edward Burne Jones") pay his respects to a dead idol, a living one, and a warm friend. Two poems, "Itylus" and "At Eleusis," are settings of classical myths. "Hendecasyllabics" is a poetic exercise on the death of summer and the onset of winter; possibly it is an allegory about the death of love and the rise of despair. Ten poems—"St. Dorothy," "The Two Dreams," "Aholibah," "Love and Sleep," "The King's Daughter," "After Death," "May Janet," "The Bloody Son," "Sea-Swallows," "The Year of Love," and "Before the Mirror"—are more or less Pre-Raphaelite in character.

These add up to eighteen poems, leaving forty-four still to be accounted for. These forty-four are the meat of the book: Among them are some of the greatest lyrics Swinburne ever wrote, lyrics which, with each passing year, emerge more and more clearly as the major basis for his fame. Among them also are the "shockers" which most clearly express his abnormal sexuality and his savage rejection of religion.

Taken together, the forty-four relate a coherent and comprehensible story. Twenty-two of them tell of a great love experience progressing through several stages. In "Hesperia" he stands in autumn on the shore of the sea, welcoming love as a bird borne on the wind from the west; this love and the beautiful sea, he hopes, will release him "from love that recalls and represses,/ That cleaves to my flesh as a flame, till the serpent has eaten his fill. . . ." [33] He confesses that he has had too much of this evil, lustful love in his life, and prays that it may not again seize his soul. Perhaps if he and the "daughter of sunset and slumber" can flee together on the swift horses of love or fear, they may escape the baneful "Lady of Pain." In "Madonna Mia," "Rondel" ("Kissing her hair I sat against her feet"), "A Match," "August," "The Sundew," and perhaps in "Love at Sea," he tells of his courtship and worship of her, apparently not without some encouragement from her. In the "Rondel," for instance, he sits against her feet kissing her hair and playfully binding her hands with the longer strands. She is his Madonna in "Madonna Mia," a poem which describes her as living in a house under apple trees and between two bowers of "Red roses full of rain," for her bondwomen are all kinds of flowers. [34]

A plaintive note is struck in "Erotion," "Satia te Sanguine," "Before Dawn," and "A Leave-Taking," though in "Erotion" (possibly for camouflage) the complaining one is a girl whose lover has rejected her and leaves her wishing for death. The deathwish motif continues and rises in acrimony in "Satia te Sanguine," in which he wishes they both were dead so that he could know whether her heart is a stone or a snake. [35] The bitterness continues in "Rococo" with his wondering what the "mad gods" will do further to vent their hatred upon him or to shower their love upon her. If she wishes, she may dream that "March may wed September"—a sneering reference to her engagement to a man twenty-one years her senior—but she will not remember nor he forget their love affair.

> *The snake that hides and hisses*
> *In heaven we twain have known;*
> *The grief of cruel kisses,*

> *The joy whose mouth makes moan;*
> *The pulse's pause and measure,*
>   *Where in one furtive vein*
> *Throbs through the heart of pleasure*
>   *The purpler blood of pain.*
>
> *We have done with tears and treasons*
>   *And love for treason's sake;*
> *Room for the swift new seasons,*
>   *The years that burn and break,*
> *Dismantle and dismember*
>   *Men's days and dreams, Juliette;**
> *For love may not remember*
>   *But time will not forget.*[36]

Acrimony gives way to a pose of defiant indifference in "Before Parting," where, gazing upon her, he marvels that he no longer loves her; her features, once so fair, now seem no longer so, and love is not even worth regretting. In "An Interlude" he recalls their love and their final parting. Now, after a lapse of time, she has forgotten his kisses and he her name. In "Félise" they meet after a year on the seashore where they had once loved and laughed. But now grown wise, he finds her no longer beautiful even though she, his "snake with bright bland eyes," now loves him and wants him to love her. But it is too late; love has vanished and cannot be recalled. Prayers and entreaties to the gods will avail nothing; for the gods are cruel and delight in scourging men. Not one dead thing have they ever restored to life, nor will they revive the dead love of Swinburne for this girl. However, he tells her cynically and ominously, it is good to look upon many loves:

> *Mutable loves, and loves perverse;*
> *But there is nothing, nor shall be,*
>   *So sweet, so wicked, but my verse*
> *Can dream of worse.*[37]

The end of this episodic love story comes in one of Swinburne's greatest and also one of his most biographically significant po-

---

* The full name of Swinburne's cousin was Mary Julia Charlotte Gordon. "Juliette" might disguise her identity from the world; she would know well enough whom Swinburne meant.

ems—"The Triumph of Time." In it his mood is nostalgic as he exclaims that had she but loved him, they would have "grown as gods. . . . Filled from the heart to the lips with love. . . ." [38] In the mood of the confessional, he adds that with her love he would have "grown pure as the dawn and the dew,/ You had grown strong as the sun or the sea." [39] But alas! She need have no fear of meeting him in heaven, he cries, for he will not be there:

> But you, had you chosen, had you stretched hand,
>   Had you seen good such a thing were done,
> I too might have stood with the souls that stand
>   In the sun's sight, clothed with the light of the sun;
> But who now on earth need care how I live?
>   Have the high gods anything left to give,
> Save dust and laurels and gold and sand?
>   Which gifts are goodly; but I will none. [40]

No, he adds, he will reject all such vanities and return to the evil life:

> Your lithe hands draw me, your face burns through me,
>   I am swift to follow you, keen to see;
> But love lacks might to redeem or undo me,
>   As I have been, I know I shall surely be;
> "What should such fellows as I do?" Nay,
>   My part were worse if I chose to play;
> For the worst is this after all; if they knew me,
>   Not a soul upon earth would pity me.
>
> And I play not for pity of these; but you,
>   If you saw with your soul what man am I,
> You would praise me at least that my soul all through
>   Clove to you, loathing the lives that lie;
> The souls and lips that are bought and sold,
>   The smiles of silver and kisses of gold,
> The lapdog loves that whine as they chew,
>   The little lovers that curse and cry. [41]

"As I have been, I know I shall surely be"—this despairing cry of a man frustrated in the one great love of his life was at once a confession and a prophecy. Leaving Mary Gordon and "North-court" in February, 1864, he journeyed to Italy to pay his respects to nonagenarian Walter Savage Landor and then returned to London. True to his promise in "Félise," he showed to what lengths he could go in his search for the "sweet" and "wicked" in his verse. "Anactoria," "Hermaphroditus," "Phaedra," "Dolores," "Faustine," "Fragoletta," "The Leper," "A Cameo," "Laus Veneris," "A Ballad of Life," "A Ballad of Death," "In the Orchard," and "Sapphics"—these poured from his pen; and, despite the misgivings of such friends as Lady Trevelyan, he insisted on their being included in *Poems and Ballads*. "Faustine," of course, had appeared in the *Spectator* in 1862, but in theme and mood it belonged with the others.

These were his *Flowers of Evil*. That Swinburne was consciously following Baudelaire's lead is manifested by the recurring image of the evil flower scattered through these poems dealing with abnormal love. In the "Ballad of Life" the sinful and voluptuous Lucrezia Borgia is described as having a mouth like a "sad red heavy rose." [42] In "Anactoria" Sappho wishes that her lips were pressed "to the bruised blossom of thy scourged white breast!"— the breast of her female love.[43] A few lines further she speaks of the "flower-sweet fingers, good to bruise or bite" and "blood like purple blossom at the tips/Quivering." In "Hermaphroditus" Swinburne asks: "To what strange end hath some strange god made fair/The double blossom of two fruitless flowers?" [44] In "Fragoletta" he exclaims:

> *Thou hast a serpent in thine hair,*
> *In all the curls that close and cling;*
> *And ah, thy breast-flower!*
> *Ah love, thy mouth too fair*
> *To kiss and sting!* [45]

"Dolores" is described as having a "cruel/Red mouth like a venomous flower." [46] He addresses her as "O mystical rose of the mire" and asks fearfully:

> *Could you hurt me, sweet lips, though I hurt you?*
> *Men touch them, and change in a trice*
> *The lilies and languors of virtue*
> *For the raptures and roses of vice;*
> *Those lie where thy foot on the floor is,*
> *These crown and caress thee and chain,*

> O splendid and sterile Dolores,
>   Our Lady of Pain.[47]

In "Sapphics" Sappho in a vision sees Aphrodite, who asks her to turn to her and normal love. Instead Sappho turns toward the Lesbian women loving each other, and sings her beautiful and terrible song.

> Then rejoiced she, laughing with love, and scattered
> Roses, awful roses of holy blossom;
> Then the Loves thronged sadly with hidden faces
>   Round Aphrodite. . . .[48]

The outcome is such that even the gods grow pale, and all flee from Sappho with revulsion, leaving the land barren and full of fruitless women. These are only a few of many such examples that could be cited, but they illustrate the Baudelairean character of the songs of abnormal love.

The "Laus Veneris," perhaps the most noted of them all, is too closely allegorical of Swinburne's unfortunate love experience to be coincidental. His version of the medieval Tannhauser story begins with the knight feasting on the evil pleasures of the Venusberg, the wicked court of Venus in the Horsel Mountain of Thuringia. Cloyed with such evil fruits, he goes to Rome to seek pardon for his sins from the Pope. But the Pontiff is so horrified at the enormity of his offenses that he tells Tannhauser there is no more possibility of his being forgiven by God than of the Pope's staff bearing a blossom. In bitter despair the knight returns to the sexual sins of Venus. The miracle of the blossoming of the papal staff takes place; but, before the news can reach Tannhauser, he has once again vanished into the sinister caverns of the Horsel Mountain. He concludes gloomily by saying that Venus will cling to him even after death, for he is cast out of God's sight until Judgment Day.

If we imagine London as the Horselberg, the life of abnormal sexual excesses there as Venus, Swinburne as Tannhauser, Mary Gordon's rejection as the Pope's, and Swinburne's return to the evil life as Tannhauser's reentry into the Venusberg, the parallel is almost perfect—almost, except for the belated forgiveness that comes with the blooming of the Pope's staff. And this is supplied, in Swinburne's case, by "Félise," with its story of Mary Gordon's too-late love of him and his scornful rejection of her because his love is dead and cannot be revived.

The only obstacle to our complete acceptance of "Laus Veneris" as the allegorical account of Swinburne's own love affair is his statement that he had completed the poem before he received Baudelaire's pamphlet on Wagner's *Tannhauser* toward the end of 1863,[49] which is tantamount to saying that the poem was finished before Mary Gordon's rejection of him in early 1864. His statement, however, may be discounted on three counts. First, he made it in his gusty *Notes on Poems and Reviews,* where he was more interested in defending *Poems and Ballads* than in telling the truth, and where his chief defense was that the poems were merely works of art and had no autobiographical significance. Second, Swinburne did not scruple to lie in order to conceal the identity of his love, as is evidenced by his telling Edmund Gosse that his love affair was with "Boo" Faulkner, rather than with Mary Gordon. Finally, his first direct allusion to the Tannhauser story occurs in his letter to Lord Houghton on March 31, 1864,[50] suggesting that he was only then planning and perhaps beginning to write "Laus Veneris." Since this was almost two months after his bitter departure from Mary Gordon, this letter—with the other evidence presented above—warrants not only setting aside Swinburne's statement that "Laus Veneris" was written before the end of 1863 but holding to our conviction that "Laus Veneris" is the poetic rendering of his unhappy love experience.

The final group of poems reject the Christian ideal of a kind and merciful God, who is loving of His children, aware of their needs, and responsive to their prayers. Among those are the "Hymn to Proserpine," "Ilicet," "A Litany," "A Lamentation," "Anima Anceps," "A Ballad of Burdens," "The Garden of Proserpine," "A Christmas Carol," "Félise," and "The Masque of Queen Bersabe." Because they also contain the idea of the rejection of God, such poems as "Anactoria" and "Laus Veneris" could have been included in this classification; but, since their chief emphasis is upon abnormal love, they are more appropriately placed in that category. "Félise," because it rejects both love and God, belongs with both the love poems and with the antitheistic group.

His mood in these poems varies from the despairing nihilism of

"Ilicet," "A Lamentation," "Anima Anceps," and "The Garden of Proserpine" to the mockery of "A Litany," "Hymn to Proserpine," "Félise," and "A Christmas Carol"—a mockery so savage that a Christian could consider it as nothing short of blasphemy. In the "Carol" and the "Litany" the mockery is subtle, the "Carol" casting the suspicion of illegitimacy on the birth of Jesus, and the "Litany" being a tongue-in-cheek satire on the cruel treatment of man by God. But in "Félise," his scorn is unmistakable when he exclaims that prayer is useless because there are no gods to hear it:

> Behold, there is no grief like this;
>   The barren blossom of thy prayer,
> Thou shalt find out how sweet it is.
>   O fools and blind, what seek ye there,
>   High up in the air?
>
> Ye must have gods, the friends of men,
>   Merciful gods, compassionate,
> And these shall answer you again.
>   Will ye beat always at the gate,
>   Ye fools of fate?
>
> Ye fools and blind; for this is sure,
>   That all ye shall not live, but die.
> Lo, what thing have you found endure?
>   Or what thing have you found on high,
>   Past the blind sky? [51]

VII   William Blake

Swinburne's interest in William Blake sprang from his association with Dante Gabriel Rossetti, who assisted his friend Alexander Gilchrist in editing the Blake manuscripts.[52] When Gilchrist took suddenly ill and died in 1861, Dante Gabriel offered to assist Gilchrist's widow in completing her husband's *Life of Blake*, and he enlisted the aid of Swinburne and William Michael Rossetti.[53] In October, 1862, Swinburne, learning that such a purist as Macmillan had been agreed upon as the publisher, refused to have anything more to do with the Gilchrist work and set about his own appreciative *William Blake*, which was ready for publication in 1866 but was delayed until January, 1868, because of the storm raised by *Poems and Ballads*.[54] In words of deep gratitude, Swinburne dedicates his book to William Michael Rossetti, dating the dedication as "November 1866." Since early in that month William had published his pamphlet *Swinburne's Poems and Ballads,* defending Swinburne in his hour of dire need in the storm that followed the publication of *Poems and Ballads,* the reason for the heartfelt tone of the dedication is obvious. Prefacing the book is a quotation from Baudelaire to the effect that all great poets are inevitably critics because it is necessary for them to examine their art, to discover its profoundest rules, and to derive from such a study the principles and guidelines which lead to perfection in the production of poetry. Baudelaire closes with the epigram that, though it is remarkable for a critic to become a poet, it is impossible for a poet not to have within him the genius of a critic.

Quite probably, this statement was the inspiration for Swinburne's own critical writings, especially this one on Blake. For what we find is not so much reasoned, objective criticism but lyrical bursts of praise. Written under the aegis of Baudelaire and Dante Gabriel Rossetti and at a time (1862-1865) when Swinburne was steeped in *l'art pour l'art,* the book is one of the most emphatic statements of the principles of "art for art's sake" in English literature. Of course he discovers in Blake a precursor of the aesthetic ideal: "To him, as to others of his kind, all faith, all virtue, all moral duty or religious necessity, was not so much abrogated or superseded as summed up, included and involved, by the one matter of art." [55] Once launched on his favorite subject, Swinburne disgresses from Blake in a fervent sermon:

The contingent result of having good art about you and living in a time of noble writing or painting may no doubt be this: that the spirit and mind of men then living will receive on some points a certain exaltation and insight caught from the influence of such forms and colours of verse or painting; will become for one thing incapable of tolerating bad work, and capable therefore of reasonably relishing the best; which of course implies and draws with it many other advantages of a sort you may call moral or spiritual. But if the artist does his work with an eye to such results or for the sake of bringing about such improvements, he will too probably fail even of them. Art for art's sake first of all, and afterwards we may suppose all the rest shall be added to her (or if not she need hardly be overmuch concerned); but from the man who falls to artistic work with a moral purpose shall be taken away even that which he has—whatever capacity for doing well in either way he may have at starting. A living critic [Baudelaire] of incomparably delicate insight and subtly good sense, himself "impeccable" as an artist, calls this "the heresy of instruction" . . . one might call it, for the sake of a shorter and more summary name, the great moral heresy. Nothing can be imagined more futile; nothing so ruinous. Once let art humble herself, plead excuses, try at any compromise with the Puritan principle of doing good, and she is worse than dead.[56]

Obviously, this statement is nothing more than a paraphrase of Baudelaire's paraphrase of Poe. Ironically, by the time Swinburne's *Blake* was published, Swinburne had done an about-face and was figuratively marching in the opposite direction by writing verses once more for the cause of Italian freedom.

VIII Love's Cross-Currents *and* Lesbia Brandon

Although Swinburne never walked down Bond Street with a red rose in hand to show his contempt for the Philistines, as Oscar Wilde did at a later date,[57] he wrote one complete novel and an extensive fragment of another for the same purpose. Even today the complete novel, first published in 1877 as *A Year's Letters* but later changed to *Love's Cross-Currents*, would be considered short, for it runs to about fifty-five thousand words. By the Victorians, so short a piece of fiction as this would not be considered a novel at all, but a tale. *Lesbia Brandon*, the fragmentary novel Swinburne wrote in spurts from 1864 into the early 1870's, runs to about seventy-five thousand words, substantially longer than *Love's Cross-Currents*, but still far short of what was considered the proper length of the novel.

I believe the significance of this matter of length is that Swinburne did not take his novels seriously, but tossed them off in the spirit of burlesque and with the idea of "poking up" the Philistines—the same spirit in which he did the fake reviews of Ernest Clouet and Félicien Cossu. Actually it would have been strange if he had taken the novel seriously as a literary form; for, though Scott had elevated at least the historical novel in Victorian esteem, the novel in general still partook of the same stigma it had acquired in medieval days by reason of its descent from the French *nouvelle*. Of course, the advent of such great Victorian novelists as Dickens, Thackeray, George Eliot, and Thomas Hardy did much to overcome traditional prejudice against the novel and to raise it to such a level of respectability that even a serious poet could turn out an occasional novel without serious loss of prestige. But this turning point was not reached till the 1880's and 1890's when Swinburne had lost interest in the novel.

In the early part of his career Swinburne used the novel exclusively for such burlesques as *La Fille du Policeman, La Soeur de la Reine,* and the fiction of flagellation which he did with Lord Houghton. In something of this same spirit he wrote *Love's Cross-Currents* and *Lesbia Brandon,* or at least he began them in this spirit, though as they developed, he, like Fielding in *Joseph Andrews,* abandoned the burlesque and took them more seriously. Likewise, as he grew older, he, like most other Victorians, acquired more respect for the novel generally. His changing attitude toward *Love's Cross-Currents* illustrates the point. On February 17, 1866, he scolded Payne of Moxon's for revealing his authorship of *Cross-Currents.*[58] In 1877 he published it under the pseudonym "Mrs. H. Manners" in installments in *The Tatler.*[59] In 1905 he published it under his own name with a dedication to Watts-Dunton, styling it as "this buried bantling of your friend's literary youth," [60] and suppressing the satirical preface with which it had appeared in *The Tatler.*

This preface of 1877 reveals clearly Swinburne's anti-Philistine design. In the form of a publisher's letter of rejection, it upbraids Mrs. Manners for impugning the sanctity of English marriages, an error of judgment into which she has fallen by living too long in immoral France. In England, the irate "publisher" continues with heavy irony, things are happily different:

Marriage in England is indissoluble, is sacred, is fortunate in every instance. Only a few—happily a very few—perverse and fanciful persons still venture to imagine or suggest that a British household can be other than the chosen home of constancy and felicity. We know, if you do not, that all husbands, all wives, and all children, born or bred or married within the boundary of the three seas, are in consequence good and happy.[61]

That she does not recognize such an obvious truth is proof of her lack of "any sufficient sense of moral beauty. Without this you can achieve no success, you can perform no work worthy of an earnest thinker in a Christian age." [62]

The satire on Philistine morality is carried out beautifully in the novel, a completely cynical tale of philandering and intrigue in an English aristocratic family like the Swinburnes and Ashburnhams. The leading character and prime mover of most of the action is old Lady Midhurst, born in 1800 and now in her early sixties; completely pagan and completely frank, she has a profound contempt for Victorian hypocrisy and prudery. Superbly intelligent and realistic, she manipulates the lives and fortunes of the other members of the family with consummate finesse and resourcefulness. Her antagonist is her niece Mrs. Clara Radworth, who, born in 1836, is a complete Victorian Philistine and a whited sepulcher. Beneath a mask of piety and altruism, she attempts to conceal a character both ruthless and devious.

The bone of contention between these two strategists is the welfare of Reginald Harewood (Swinburne himself) and his half-sister Amicia Cheyne, wife of Lord Cheyne. Both grandchildren of Lady Midhurst, they are the objects of her affection and concern. During the course of the story, Reginald becomes involved in a love affair with Mrs. Clara Radworth, who, outwardly pretending to resist his affections, subtly draws him on. Sensing the potential damage to Reginald from such an affair and divining the true role of Clara, Lady Midhurst strives unsuccessfully to free him from the clutches of her niece. When she finally comes into possession of a packet of letters revealing a former love affair of Clara's with a French philanderer named M. de Saverny, she threatens to send them to Reginald unless Clara crushes his love for her with a cold, blunt statement that she wishes to have no more to do with him. This Clara does.

The other strand of the plot concerns the story of Amicia, married lovelessly and childlessly to the Philistine humanitarian, Lord Cheyne. Frank Cheyne, Clara Radworth's brother, visits Lord Cheyne and Amicia at "Lidcombe," the family seat. Frank and his cousin Amicia, reviving their old love affair, commit adultery; almost immediately afterward Lord Cheyne drowns accidentally. Lord Cheyne's death without issue leaves Frank heir to the family title. In due course the widowed Amicia leaves "Lidcombe," and Frank takes possession as the new Lord Cheyne. Triumphant because her brother has replaced Amicia's husband

in the title, Clara Radworth writes Lady Midhurst a letter over-
flowing with malicious sympathy.

Then comes the catastrophe. Lady Midhurst lets it be known
that Amicia is pregnant. In due course she gives birth to a son
whom all the family know to be Frank's; but, for the sake of
family honor, they dare not say so. This illegitimate child is therefore recognized as Lord Cheyne's son and as the proper heir to
the title. Frank, through his adulterous act, has cheated himself of
his birthright. There is nothing else for him to do but to resign
the title and move from "Lidcombe." He does so, and Amicia and
her infant heir take possession. Clara's triumph over Lady Midhurst and her granddaughter is therefore short lived. Lady Midhurst quickly seizes the opportunity to even the score with Clara
by writing her a letter in which the venom and *double entendre*
are masterfully injected. So skillfully does Swinburne weave together the threads of his narrative that it is the same letter in
which she tells Clara of the acquisition of her love letters to the
Frenchman, by means of which she forces her to dismiss Reginald.
Not satisfied even with this, the ruthless old campaigner visits
Clara and gloats over her chagrin, conveying her impressions to
Amicia with relish in her letter which is the concluding one of
the novel:

They get on well enough again by this time, I believe. To use her own
style, she is *dead beat,* and quite safe; viciously resigned. I think we
may look for peace. She would have me racked if she could, no doubt,
but received me smiling from the tips of her teeth outwards, and with
a soft dry pressure of the fingers. Not a hint of anything kept back.
Evidently, too, she holds her brother well in leash. Frank pleased me:
he was courteous, quiet, without any sort of affectation, dissembled or
displayed.[63]

Lady Midhurst is of course the great creation of the story and
one of the great characters of fiction; she is worthy of standing
beside Becky Sharp, Lady Castlewood, and Elizabeth Bennet.
The English novel has nobody quite like her, though Miss Craw-
ley in *Vanity Fair* is cut from the same stout oak. Her character
does not change during the story, but it is of such complexity and
depth that it would be an achievement for any novel. For a work
as short as *Love's Cross-Currents* and for one so restricted by the

limitations of the epistolary style, her portrait is truly a work of great art. She is not only Swinburne's spokesman for "art for art's sake" in her frequent gibes at the affectations of moral and religious hypocrites, but is Swinburne himself in her paganism and religious nihilism. And yet she is still more: fierce old virago though she is, she epitomizes the indomitable British courage which conquered Napoleon's battalions and shot Hitler's Luftwaffe out of the skies. In words reminiscent of Churchill's "blood, sweat, and tears," she writes to Amicia, who is distraught and conscience stricken after the death of Lord Cheyne:

I could wish to write you a softer-toned letter of comfort than this; but one thing I must say: do not let your grief hurry you even for one minute beyond the reach of advice. As for comfort, my dearest child, what can I well say? I have always hated condolence myself: where it is anything, it is bad—helpless and senseless at best. A grievous thing has happened; we can say no more when all comment has been run through. To us for some time—I say to us, callous as you are now thinking me—the loss and misfortune will seem even greater than they are. You have the worst of it. Nevertheless, it is not the end of all things. The world will dispense with us some day; but it shall not while we can hold out. Things must go on when we have dropped off; but, while we can, let us keep up with life.[64]

Lesbia Brandon shows the effects of being written during Swinburne's dark period after the unfortunate love affair with Mary Gordon. In the mood and spirit of the worst poems of *Poems and Ballads*—to which it has many similarities—and of the most frenetic scenes of *Chastelard*, this novel is a prose *Flowers of Evil*. Swinburne's purpose in it also was to roil the Philistine, but in a much more coarse and brutal fashion than in *Love's Cross-Currents*. In January, 1867, while he was still smarting from the debacle of *Poems and Ballads*, he wrote Richard Burton: "I have in hand a scheme of mixed verse and prose—a sort of étude à la Balzac *plus* the poetry—which I flatter myself will be more offensive and objectionable to Britannia than anything I have yet done. You see I have now a character to keep up, and by the grace of Cotytto I will endeavour not to come short of it—at least in my writings." [65]

Although longer than *Love's Cross-Currents, Lesbia* is so fragmentary that the reader is hard put to make a coherent story of it.

Swinburne introduces himself into this novel also—as Bertie Seyton, who at the beginning is a youngster prepping for Eton chiefly by being flogged by his psychotic tutor Denham. Besides flagellation, the novel offers other evidences of abnormal sexuality in the suggestion of incestuous love between Bertie and his sister Lady Wariston and between Lady Wariston and Tutor Denham, who turns out to be her and Bertie's half-brother. Lesbianism enters the story with the name "Lesbia Brandon." Lesbia is a soulless beauty lacking femininity, who is like Atalanta, Mary Stuart, or perhaps Mary Gordon as Swinburne describes her in some of the love poems of *Poems and Ballads*. Homosexuality is present in Bertie Seyton, who Swinburne said was himself, who enjoys being flogged, dresses up in girls' clothes, and is described as having such "a strong feminine element" that ". . . he ought to have been a pretty . . . girl." [66]

Significantly, as Bertie matures, he falls in love with the strange creature, Lesbia Brandon, who, like Mary Gordon, is interested in writing, though she writes verse rather than fiction. But, when he presses his suit, he suffers the same fate described in "The Triumph of Time," "Satia te Sanguine," "A Leave-Taking," and several others of *Poems and Ballads*. Sadly she tells him she would love and marry him if she could love and marry anyone, but she is unmarriageable. Henceforth they must be as brother and sister, not lovers.

Lesbia commits suicide through the prolonged use of eau de cologne and opium. Bertie sits by her bed as she describes a dream which bears a strong resemblance to "The Garden of Proserpine." In her dream Lesbia sees Proserpine standing in a field of poppies and surrounded by ghostly figures. Sympathetically, Bertie holds Lesbia's hand until she finishes the story of her dream. Addressing him as her brother, she wonders what love with him would have been like, and she asks him to kiss her. As he does so, he loses control and kisses her so violently that she pushes him away and begs him to let her die in peace. Subdued, he sits till dawn; then she bids him goodby, turns her face to the pillow, and dies.

One thing is certain: In *Lesbia Brandon*, as in *Chastelard* and in *Poems and Ballads*, Swinburne was doing more than baiting the Philistines; he was expressing and exhibiting the abnormal side of his nature, the side to which, as he had threatened in

Poems and Ballads, he would give free rein as a retaliatory measure for his defeat in love. Such a reaction by the person abnormally inclined is entirely in accord with the findings of Dr. Bieber and his associates in the study we have referred to before. Homosexual proclivities being at variance with nature, the victim is impelled by nature, at various times in his life, to reach for normalcy. If the attempt meets with frustration, he falls back all the more deeply and hopelessly into abnormality. Such a reach did Swinburne make toward Mary Gordon; *Chastelard, Poems and Ballads,* and *Lesbia Brandon* are the fruits of his defeat.

In *Love's Cross-Currents* and in *Lesbia Brandon* Swinburne proved that he could have been a very good or perhaps a very great novelist. He would have had to work at the craft, for he obviously had much to learn. The cumbersome "Prologue" to *Love's Cross-Currents* is so obscure that the reader needs a character chart to straighten out the interrelationships of the characters, while the ill-advised use of the epistolary framework precludes necessary comments and interpretations by the author. Still, both novels have an immediacy, a skillful handling of scene and dialogue, depth of understanding of life, and an ability to portray character that indicate talents of a high order. The only obstacle lying athwart the path of success was that his interests lay in other directions.

CHAPTER 6

Turnabout

THE literary detonation following immediately upon the publication of *Poems and Ballads* was the greatest in England since the days of Byron and Shelley. The proliferation of magazines and newspapers brought about during the 1830's and 1840's by the improvements in printing added many journalistic voices to the harsh chorus that burst forth in condemnation of Swinburne's book.

As it happened, the first blasts at *Poems and Ballads* came to him in a fashion both dramatic and unfortunate. Out strolling with Bertram Payne, head of Moxon's publishing house since the death of Moxon, Swinburne saw the issue of the *Saturday Review* for August 4, 1866, bought it, and read it while standing in the street. So furious did he become and so violent was his language that Payne steered him into a tea room, begging him to do his cursing in French.

Within a day or so, Payne discontinued the publication and circulation of *Poems and Ballads*. Sir William Hardman, a publisher himself, quotes a rumor that Dallas of *The Times* notified Payne that he had written an article denouncing both Swinburne and Payne, that the article was already in type, and that it would be printed in the "Thunderer" shortly unless Payne killed the book.[1] Payne, fearful that such a denunciation from such an august source might lead to prosecution and humiliation, stopped publication immediately.

The story might be true, or it might be an invention of Payne's, who was not overly scrupulous and who might have invented it as an excuse for his breach of contract with Swinburne. For a breach of contract it was. The proper time for Payne to have demurred and to have demanded the excision of questionable material from the book was before he accepted it for publication. As the publisher of *Chastelard*, he not only knew the bent that Swinburne's work was taking, but was also aware of the unfavorable reaction it had stirred up. If he had doubts of his own judgment, he could have done what Chapman did earlier when the manuscript of *Poems and Ballads* was submitted to him—consulted Browning or someone equally qualified to judge it.[2]

One other possibility deserves consideration in this matter. Moxon's was also the publisher for Tennyson, the Laureate. Tennyson's condemnation of *Chastelard* had been so emphatic that we can imagine his choler when he read *Poems and Ballads*. He could have written Payne a note or else have stormed into his office demanding the discontinuance of the offending book on the threat of transferring his patronage to another publisher if it were not done. And, of course, Tennyson would have insisted that Payne not mention his name as the reason for the withdrawal.

Two facts suggest Tennyson's connection with Payne's decision: A short two years later, Tennyson did break with Moxon's and made an agreement with the eminently proper Alexander Strahan to publish him. Even before Payne announced his decision to withdraw Swinburne's book, the bruised and smarting Swinburne received an invitation from Edward Bulwer-Lytton to visit him at "Knebworth." [3] And the invitation came to Swinburne on August 4, the day when the blow fell. Curiously enough, no close tie existed between Swinburne and Lytton; in fact, before the invitation only two other letters between the two are recorded: one from Lytton to Swinburne, congratulating him on *Atalanta*, and a grateful response from Swinburne on January 16, 1866.[4]

On the other hand, no love existed between Tennyson and Lytton. Promoted by a mutual antipathy, the two men satirized each other publicly and privately, making no attempt to conceal their disdain. Since *Poems and Ballads* was published about July 16, 1866, it is possible that Lytton had heard through the literary grapevine of Tennyson's angry fulminations and of the inimical reviews shortly to appear, suspected that Tennyson was one of the instigators of the reviews, and decided to aid the victim. At any rate, the arrival of Lytton's invitation simultaneously with the appearance of the reviews in the *Saturday* and the *Athenaeum* is a singular coincidence unless he was in London on that day, read the review, dashed off a note, and sent it immediately.

The review in the *Saturday* was by John Morley, later Lord Morley, who in 1866 was twenty-eight, one year younger than Swinburne. A disciple of John Stuart Mill and an agnostic, as well as something of a snob, Morley had turned to journalism when his father, angry because his son would not become an Anglican clergyman, cut off his allowance.[5] Quite possibly, Morley's savage review was at least partially the result of the views of John Douglas Cook, editor, Tory, and High Church Anglican, and of the Reverend William Scott, assistant editor and High Churchman also.[6] Certainly it was in accordance with the Tory character of the *Saturday*, which, though it had been founded as recently as 1855 by Beresford Hope, represented the ultraconservative viewpoint.[7]

Morley's review runs over two thousand words and is tinged with heavy irony. Implicit in it is the suggestion that Swinburne was a homosexual who could not help dwelling on the unnatural aspects of sex.[8] Admitting the futility of lecturing any artist on his material, Morley says Swinburne has to go in the direction his "character" forces him: "If the character of his genius drives him pretty exclusively in the direction of libidinous song, we may be very sorry, but it is of no use to advise him and preach to him. What comes of discoursing to a fiery tropical flower of the pleasant fragrance of the rose or the fruitfulness of the fig-tree?" [9]

With an ironic shrug of the shoulders he continues: "It is of no use, therefore, to scold Mr. Swinburne for grovelling down among the shameless abominations which inspire him with such frensied delight. They excite his imagination to its most vigorous efforts, they seem to him the themes the most proper for poetic treatment, and they suggest ideas which, in his opinion, it is highly to be wished that English men and women should brood upon and make their own." [10]

Then, mockingly, he affects to praise his victim, but actually he scorns him for revealing his abnormality: "And at all events he deserves credit for the audacious courage with which he has revealed to the world a mind all aflame with the feverish carnality of a schoolboy over the dirtiest passages in Lemprière. It is not every poet who would ask us to go hear him tuning his lyre in a stye. It is not everybody who would care to let the world know that he found the most delicious food for poetic reflection in the practices of the great island of the Aegean, in the habits of Messalina, of Faustina, of Pasiphäe." [11]

Morley drops the mask of sympathy to say that, if Swinburne had rebelled only against the prudes, no one would find fault with him. "But there is an enormous difference between an attempt to revivify among us the grand old pagan conceptions of Joy, and an attempt to glorify all the bestial delights that the subtleness of Greek depravity was able to contrive." [12]

Unquestionably, Morley's is one of the great reviews in English literary history. Its length, artistry, and subtlety indicate that he had worked on it for a week or two at least. One can readily see why it drove Swinburne into a frenzy: he could not have failed to understand the veiled allusions and to realize that perceptive readers would likewise understand them.

Like Morley's, Buchanan's review in the *Athenaeum* contains the implication of homosexuality, but, couched in classical terms, its full meaning would have been understood only by the well educated.[13] Buchanan must have been aware of Swinburne's abhorrence of being called boyish, for he remarks patronizingly that these poems are too puerile to do any serious moral damage to anybody because they are so insincere and affected. Then, like a rapier thrust to the vitals, comes the damaging allusion: "They are too juvenile and unreal for that. The strong pulse of true passion beats in no one of them. They are unclean, with little power; and uncleanness repulses. Here, in fact, we have Gito, seated in the tub of Diogenes, conscious of the filth and whining at the stars." [14]

Now in the ancient Roman novel, the *Satyricon,* written by Petronius Arbiter, one of the prominent officials at the court of Nero, Gito is the boy with whom the narrator Encolpius has sexual relations. This was not uncommon among the ancients. Only now is the *Satyricon* easy to get here, but in England in 1862 a German edition of it is advertised in the respectable *Publishers' Circular*. It is safe to assume that Swinburne was familiar with it, what with his wide classical reading at Oxford and his browsing in Lord Houghton's library at Fryston. It is equally safe to assume that most of the Victorian intelligentsia who were male and university educated would get the full drift of the Gito reference. Buchanan's article ends significantly with advice that Swinburne should "cast his evil advisers aside" and turn to wisdom. After this book, Buchanan predicts, even the "parasites" will avoid him; and the best course for him is to "seek out Nature" and to "try to think seriously on life and art." [15]

The reference to the "evil advisers" and to Swinburne as Gito shows that Buchanan was well informed about the facts of Swinburne's private life. As Lady Trevelyan had warned Swinburne, his wild and loose talk in gatherings of literary men had given him a bad reputation that did him no good now. A person in private life may get away with all manner of immorality without news of it getting about, but writers, actors, and outstanding politicians are regarded as public property, and word of their shenanigans soon becomes universal knowledge.

Almost the next day after Payne announced his withdrawal of *Poems and Ballads,* Dante Gabriel Rossetti and Frederick Sandys called on him in an effort to persuade him to reconsider. He was, they reported, so terrified at the prospect of prosecution that their efforts were in vain. Swinburne availed himself of Bulwer-Lytton's invitation to withdraw from the London scene to think. Enraged at Payne's breach of contract, he was determined to republish *Poems and Ballads* without any changes. To do anything else, he wrote Lord Lytton, would be deserting his colors.[16] But how? Who would now take it, a foundling of evil repute?

Through the offices of either Howell, Lord Houghton, or perhaps Joseph Knight, he entered into an agreement with an unsavory publisher, John Camden Hotten, who had built his business largely on the publishing and selling of pornographic books to a carefully selected clientele. Hotten paid Swinburne £200 for the first thousand copies of *Poems and Ballads,* bought up the remainder of Moxon's unsold stock, and reissued the book around November 1, 1866.[17] Before doing so, he persuaded Swinburne to write and publish a pamphlet, *Notes on Poems and Reviews,* in which he defended himself against the charges hurled against him on the ground that his poems in *Poems and Ballads* were objective studies and commentaries, not the expression of his personal opinion or belief. "Hermaphroditus," for instance, was simply a study of the statue in the Louvre, nothing more, and "Laus

Veneris" was a new treatment of an old medieval legend. That the reviewers had discerned anything objectionable in such poems was evidence only of their own evil minds.

Simultaneously with Swinburne's defense, Hotten published also William Rossetti's lengthy essay, *Swinburne's Poems and Ballads,* which he had first hoped to publish in the *North American Review.* It was rejected there, largely through the influence of James Russell Lowell, who had published in that journal strongly disapproving reviews of *Chastelard* and *Poems and Ballads.* Few men have ever surpassed William Rossetti in the art of seeming to say something without saying it, of casting aspersions and vicious suggestions while apparently striving to be fair and impartial. Likewise, when he wanted to be, he was a master at obfuscating an issue or a question. His essay begins with the bland statement that his purpose is to examine Swinburne's poems in order to assign him his proper place among poets—a high place, Rossetti feels certain. The so-called "indecencies" of *Poems and Ballads* he finds to be only literary frankness on classical subjects, a line of argument close to Swinburne's and as specious; for William Rossetti knew as well as did Swinburne that the objectionable poems were largely autobiographical. Answering the charges of indecency, he delivers this piece of gobbledygook: "Of positive grossness or foulness of expression there is none—nor yet of light-hearted, jocular, jovial libertinism. The offences to decency are in the subjects selected—sometimes too faithfully classic, sometimes more or less modern or semiabstract —and in the strength of phrase which the writer insists upon using on these as on other topics." [18]

These circuitous defenses might have fooled the gullible—but not anybody who had read *Poems and Ballads* with understanding. Under the caption "Calling a Thing by its Right Name," *Punch* lived up to its name with this heavy blow: "Having read Mr. Swinburne's defence of his prurient poetics, *Punch* hereby gives him his royal licence to change his name to what is evidently its true form—SWINEBORN." [19]

Many more notices appeared in the press, but their tenor followed generally the lead of the *Saturday* and the *Athenaeum.* Here and there a friend raised his voice to try to stem the tide of condemnation, as Lord Houghton did in an unsigned letter to the *Examiner;*[20] but such attempts only brought forth even more harsh rejoinders such as Carleton Greene's in the Cambridge University magazine, *The Light Blue.*[21]

The effect on Swinburne of his catastrophe and of all the obloquy heaped upon his name can be imagined. He had become increasingly bolder in the expression of the abnormal side of his nature because of the encouragement of such people as Dante Rossetti and Lord Houghton—despite their denials, they did encourage him, as is borne out by the accounts of Henry Adams, William Hardman, and Lady Ritchie. Association with such men as Charles Howell and Simeon Solomon had increased his boldness because it dispelled any lingering doubts he might have had as to the necessity of restraining and concealing his abnormality. And of course, as we have already noted, the doctrine of "art for art's sake," supported by the example of Baudelaire's *Les Fleurs du Mal,* had given him a complete rationale for letting himself go.

He had done just this. He had told the secret longings of his soul; he had laid bare the tragedy of his personal defeat in love; and what had happened? The friends who had encouraged him, on whom he had counted, had withdrawn from him: Lord Houghton betook himself to Vichy; Meredith was away; the Rossettis were at best lukewarm. Swinburne was left to fight alone in a joyless battle in which even a partial victory brought him small satisfaction. True, he had succeeded in republishing *Poems and Ballads,* but, to do so, he had been forced into association with the disreputable Hotten and to resort to a mass of lies—and what he and his friends well knew were lies—in his *Notes.* The whole affair caused him untold anguish.

Nor can we forget that this man did not stand alone in his suffering. A member of two of England's old aristocratic families and bearing a proud old name, he could not be unmindful that many others were affected by what happened to him, especially anything as disgraceful as this. We can imagine the letters that flitted around among the Swinburnes and Ashburnhams at the spectacle that Cousin Hadji was making of himself in London. We can imagine, too, the angry letters that came to him from his harassed parents, uncles, aunts, and cousins because of the humiliation he had brought upon them.

Rumors persist that, shortly after the republication of *Poems and Ballads,* a conference atended by Jowett and others took place to discuss what had best be done with Swinburne. I think it much more likely that it was a conference at "Holmwood" during the Christmas season, when the Swinburnes always gathered anyway, and that it was attended principally by the Admiral, Lady Jane, Swinburne, and possibly an uncle or aunt. I believe that what we know of Swinburne provides us with ample material for a conjecture on how they handled the problem of stopping him in his mad career and of turning him into safer channels.

To have threatened, scolded, and commanded would have only made him more rebellious. But Lady Jane knew her son, his love for her, and his pride in his name and family. All she would have had to do would be to point to the ignominious sneer in *Punch* to illustrate the damage he was doing them all. Then she could remind him that any marriage prospects his sisters Alice, Charlotte, and Isabel—all at home and in their middle or late twenties—might have would be worsened or perhaps ruined forever by his antics. I think it highly possible that the Admiral added a flat warning that unless Swinburne changed his literary course, he would discontinue the £200 he had been giving him every year. Without this money and with now no certain prospect of literary earnings, Swinburne could hardly have continued in London.

The Admiral and Lady Jane could have pointed out to him that his name was a proud one because of the luster his ancestors had given it, luster he could add to or detract from by his own life and work. Such considerations were enough, I believe, to make him pause to reconsider the course of his career and perhaps to give at least a halfway promise that he would stir up no more hornets' nests right away.

But it is not enough to take something away; something must be added to take its place. If such idols as Dante Rossetti and Lord Houghton were overturned and if the old religion of "art for art's sake" were abandoned, what was to fill the void? The ideal of republicanism had never been completely forgotten, but it had been thrust into the background by de Sadism and aestheticism. Italy was still struggling for her freedom against the forces of reaction, and France still lived under the autocratic rule of Napoleon III. As early as October 9, 1866, Swinburne wrote William Rossetti that, after many months of inactivity, he was able to write verse again and was working on his "A Song of Italy" in which he intended to express his reverence for Mazzini. He added: "After all, in spite of jokes and perversities . . . it is nice to have something to love and to believe in as I do in Italy." [22]

Nor had his enthusiasm for Victor Hugo and for the cause of French republicanism ever waned. His review of *Les Miserables* in the *Spectator* had led to exchanges of complimentary letters with Hugo and to the dedication of *Chastelard* to him. He fed his mind with Hugo's thought and philosophy, eagerly devouring each new work as soon as it came out. From Hugo's *Les Contemplations* and from the first part of his *La Légende des Siècles* (1859), Swinburne made his first acquaintanceship with Auguste Comte's Positivism, a philosophy which came prominently to the fore in England in the middle and late 1860's, largely through the writings of John Stuart Mill and of Harriet Martineau, who translated Comte's *Cours de Philosophie Positive* in 1852. Briefly put, Comte's Positivism denies the existence of a personal God, metaphysics, and revealed religion, and sets up humanity as God. Through his intelligence, man will in time solve all his problems and achieve a utopian civilization on earth. The shackles which have held man back and retarded his progress through the ages are the kings and priests who enslaved man's mind and robbed him of his freedom. All human history is but the story of how man, slowly and painfully, has broken one bond after another as he has plodded upward. Though much has been done, much remains to do; and the duty of the Positivist is to expound his doctrines to the ignorant masses so as to dispel darkness and hasten the advent of the Positivist heaven.

Essentially this was the philosophy Hugo expounded in *Les Contemplations* and in the first part of *La Légende des Siècles.* Swinburne seems not to have fully grasped the philosophy when he published his article "Victor Hugo's Philosophy" in the *Spectator* in 1862, for he complains therein that Hugo will not accept human meanness or adopt any philosophy which accepts it. Actually, Hugo's Positivism accepts human perversity as the evil against which man struggles but which he finally conquers. However, Swinburne soon comprehended and accepted the tenets of Positivism, for in "A Song of Italy," read to Mazzini at the end of March, 1867, Positivistic thought is unmistakable in the depiction of kings' wailing and priests' growing pale before the advent of freedom.

Postivism was easy for Swinburne to turn to because it included much that he already believed, as well as adding some new and optimistic touches which, as he wrote William Rossetti, were a welcome relief to the cheerless nihilism and despair under which he had lived for the past ten years. It commanded him to despise any form of political tyranny; it scorned Christianity and other forms of religion as mere absurd superstitions; it gave him a God in which he could believe, the limitless possibilities of man's intellect; it promised him a final great day of triumph in the future. After the bleak despair of pagan nihilism he had expressed in such poems as "Laus Veneris," "Anactoria," and "The Garden of Proserpine," he must have felt like one who had come out of a dank mausoleum into the warm sunshine.

Events shaped themselves so opportunely toward the new end that we cannot throw off the suspicion that the Admiral and Lady Jane did enlist the aid of Jowett and perhaps, through him, Aurelio Saffi—a former associate of Mazzini and Swinburne's old Italian teacher at Oxford—to supply the one ingredient necessary to complete his conversion: an idol. The idol came forward in the person of Mazzini, who on March 10, 1867, wrote Swinburne a belated thanks for the gift copy of *Atalanta* he had received two years earlier but had never acknowledged, praised his recently published "Ode to Candia," and included a fervent piece of rhetoric urging him to abandon "songs of egotistical love and idolatry of physical beauty" and to turn out "a series of 'Lyrics for the Crusade.'" [23]

Things progressed rapidly. On March 30, 1867, Swinburne, all atremble, went with his friend Thomas Purnell to the house of Karl Blind, a German exile, and waited in a crowded room until the great man entered. As Swinburne wrote his mother next day, Mazzini walked up to him, said, "I know you," and Swinburne went down on his knees, seized the idol's hand, and kissed it. Then he read him "A Song of Italy," which Mazzini praised highly, inviting the poet to call on him whenever he wished. The conversion was an accomplished fact.

I *A Song of Italy*

Mazzini commented to Swinburne, after he had finished reading the poem, that there was too much about him in it. We are bound to admit that he is right. A poem of some 840 lines, almost a third of it is in praise of "the Chief," as Swinburne calls him;

and the chorus of praise rises until it becomes an ecstatic litany, calling upon the Italian cities to praise Mazzini as the savior. We can imagine that Mazzini went through an ordeal in that crowded room as he listened to the singsong voice of Swinburne apotheosizing him. In alternating lines of iambic pentameter and trimeter with each two lines rhyming, the poem is much longer than it needs to be and has too much use of alliteration.

The effect upon the reader is one of tedium. We suspect that the poet was trying to huff and puff himself into an emotion which he did not really feel and to cover up with words a barrenness of feeling and a poverty of thought. It is almost as if Swinburne has turned the clock back to his early days at Oxford and the "Ode to Mazzini."

II Songs before Sunrise

The *Songs before Sunrise* are based on the hope of both Mazzini and Swinburne that Italian freedom would grow out of the repudiation of any form of monarchy and of the temporal power of the Pope, and that the form of government finally set up would be republican. By 1867, when Swinburne met Mazzini, King Victor Emmanuel had secured control of almost all of Italy with the exception of Rome. Mazzini's hope was that Rome would be the nucleus of the republic, and that the republican spirit would then spread over all Italy and unseat the monarchy. This, of course, did not take place until the mid-twentieth century, following World War II, when Umberto was denied the throne and Italy became what she is today—a republic.

Mazzini's and Swinburne's dream of an Italian republic was doomed because they were a century ahead of their time. The Italians wished to be rid of foreign intervention and exploitation, but they had for so many centuries been used to monarchical government that the extent of their desires was only to supplant the foreign monarch with one of their own, not to do away with the system altogether. Likewise, although they had long been cynical toward the temporal aspects of the papacy and the governmental structure of the Catholic Church, they had no doctrinal quarrel with it, and no thought of repudiating it, as Swinburne and many other Englishmen hoped.

Had Swinburne fully realized the innate conservatism of the Italian people, his enthusiasm would have been considerably lessened. As it was, he plunged into the cause with all the verve of a zealot. In the "Dedication" to Mazzini he sings: "I bring you the sword of a song,/ The sword of my spirit's desire. . . ." [24] Plainly he saw himself as a warrior in verse, perhaps something of a vicarious realization of an ideal as old as his youthful desire to become a soldier in the Crimean War. He must have been aware that he had done a complete about-face from the principles of "art for art's sake," for as a verse-soldier he was writing poetry to serve a cause.

He carries this militant spirit into the "Prelude," a poetic repudiation of *Poems and Ballads*. The "fierce flute," the cymbal, and the "clamorous kettledrum" that had once acclaimed "dim goddesses of fiery fame" are now silent; pleasure and passion have passed and there yet remains

> *A little time that we may fill*
> *Or with such good works or such ill*
> *As loose the bonds or make them strong*
> *Wherein all manhood suffers wrong.*[25]

His first "good work" was "Super Flumina Babylonis," a poem in honor of Mazzini's manifesto of 1831 to "Young Italy," calling upon youth to rise in the cause of liberty. The weeping "by the waters of Babylon" gives way to triumphant joy as the light of freedom dawns. The mood changes to one of grief for the capture of Garibaldi by Rattazzi in September, 1867. England is blamed for her indifference and the Pope execrated for perfidy, while Garibaldi, who had escaped before the poem could be published, is reminded that his name will be famous in free Italy.

Two poems sound the strong note of Postivism: "Hertha," which Swinburne considered the best verse he had ever written, and the "Hymn of Man," a solemn note of warning on the occasion of the Ecumenical Council of 1870. Hertha, the old German goddess of the earth, represents growth or nature. In language borrowed from the Book of Job, she says:

> *Before ever land was,*
> *Before ever the sea,*
> *Or soft hair of the grass,*
> *Or fair limbs of the tree,*
> *Or the flesh-coloured fruit of my branches, I was, and thy soul was in*
> *me.*[26]

God speaks, but He is a Positivist God who comdemns as false all other concepts of Him; He does not need prayer or supplication; His only command is to live. But He sadly upbraids men for worshiping false gods and for neglecting Him. He closes with a proclamation that He and man are identical:

> *One birth of my bosom;*
> *One beam of mine eye;*
> *One topmost blossom*
> *That scales the sky;*
> *Man, equal and one with me, man that is made of me, man that is I.*[27]

"The Hymn of Man" jeers at the heads of the Catholic Church for having created God for their own sakes, and warns them that their God is about to die the same death that all false gods have suffered. In "Before a Crucifix" and in "Tenebrae" Swinburne also uses the terminology of Catholicism to condemn Christianity and to extol Positivism—much in the same fashion that he had done in the most blasphemous poems of *Poems and Ballads*. The chief difference is that there is no reference to sex in the *Songs before Sunrise*.

France comes in for a share of attention in "Mater Dolorosa," "Mater Triumphalis," and "A Marching Song"—in all of which the poet grieves that the mother of freedom is content to sit in bondage. But in the "Ode on the Proclamation of the French Republic," dated September 4, 1870, his joy is delirious with the realization of his dreams.

Included among the *Songs* is "To Walt Whitman in America," asking the American poet to send overseas a song of freedom to Englishmen too steeped in greed and error to compose such songs for themselves; and "Cor Cordium," a sonnet in tribute to Shelley, "for whom / The lyrist liberty made life a lyre." [28] The sentiment is sincere and beautiful; the verse suffers from too much alliteration.

The final item in the volume of the Bonchurch Edition containing the *Songs* is a series of seventeen sonnets, most of which were published in the *Examiner* during 1873. As savage as anything Swinburne ever wrote, they underscore the fact that Positivism had not extinguished his love of invective. They consign to hell such of his pet hates as Ferdinand II, Pius IX, and Napoleon III,

over whom he gives thanks that he has lived long enough to say,
". . . The dog is dead." [29] The seventeenth sonnet is titled
"Apologia." The bitterness of his verse, he says, is not his fault,
but theirs whose wrongdoings have raised such bitterness within
him.

Right here might be the place to point out the complete lack of
compassion in Swinburne's poems. A great poet, ever mindful of
the essential tragedy of human life, has a measure of pity even
for an Iago, a Pardoner, a Creon, or a Satan. And most men are so
keenly conscious of their own faults that they can view the sins of
others with some tolerance and even forgiveness, if not before, at
least after their deaths. Swinburne was curiously incapable of
such tolerance and forgiveness, even long years after the dissolu-
tion of those he had hated.

CHAPTER 7

The Literary Gamecock

IN ALL cases Swinburne's literary quarrels came about because of his inability to believe that criticism of him and his works could ever be impartial and objective. In his view, critics were either friends or enemies: If friends, they praised; if enemies, they attacked. There was no middle ground.

In part, of course, this conviction came from the peculiarities of his own history and temperament. But in great part it came from an awareness of the puffery and antipuffery underlying much of Victorian reviewing. Biographies of such literary figures as Tennyson, Thackeray, Dante Rossetti, Robert Buchanan, and Thomas Hardy, to mention only a few, offer ample testimony that the Victorian reviewer was often motivated by considerations other than literary merit and demerit. This is not to say that honest criticism did not exist, for it did, and to a remarkable extent; but too often it existed side by side with mercenary criticism.

Toward the end of his *Notes on Poems and Reviews* Swinburne says: "I have never been able to see what should attract men to the profession of criticism but the noble pleasure of praising." [1] He was probably not fully aware that he did not practice his own rule; for, even when engaged in praising, as in the *Blake*, he could not forbear making invidious comparisons to the disadvantage of others. It is safe to assume that he followed the same procedure in his verbal remarks, often more dangerous than the written in that they are not usually pondered over beforehand and cannot be erased afterward.

Throughout his career his criticisms of others and theirs of him involved him in a series of imbroglios that he could well have done without. Besides the quarrel with Hutton of the *Spectator* that we have already mentioned, he had brushes with George

Eliot, Dr. Furnivall of the New Shakespeare Society, Emerson, Browning, Lowell, and his old friend Whistler; and, aligned with William and Dante Rossetti, Swinburne engaged in a prolonged and climactic quarrel with Robert Buchanan in the Fleshly Controversy, one of the most far-reaching and significant literary wars in English literary history. The others we can pass by with mere mention; the Fleshly Controversy, because of its profound significance to Swinburne's life and writings, deserves full treatment.

I *The Fleshly Controversy*

We do not know the initial cause of the ill feeling between Robert Buchanan and Swinburne, but it could not have been Payne's taking from Buchanan and giving to Swinburne the edition of Keats for which Buchanan had already written an introduction. Swinburne's letter of January 4, 1866, to William Rossetti on the matter shows that even then he had no love for the Scotsman. Recounting Payne's proposal that he take over the edition for £10, the amount already paid Buchanan, Swinburne says with evident malice: "This sum the publisher is willing to lose, and to cancel the poor devil's work, if I will do Keats instead on those terms: and won't I? and wouldn't I gratis? This forthcoming Scotch edition of Keats, who hated the Scotch as much as I do . . . has long been a thorn in my side: and apart from the delight of trampling on a Scotch Poetaster, I shall greatly enjoy bringing out a perfect edition of Keats with all his good verses and none of his bad." [2]

A curious mixture of feelings is evinced here. He has a grain of sympathy for Buchanan because of the loss of the edition, but he scorns him as a Scot and rejoices that Keats is out of his hands. The personal note implies that the two had met, perhaps at a gathering at Moxon's; had found each other distasteful; but were not active enemies. In his letter to Payne on January 5, 1867, Swinburne insists that Payne make it clear to Buchanan that the transfer of the Keats was in no way Swinburne's doing but had been done by Payne without any request or suggestion from Swinburne. Evidently he was apprehensive of reprisals. He had good reason to be, for Buchanan was also redheaded, short tempered, and as quick to take offence as Swinburne.

Born in 1841 of humble Scottish-Welsh parentage, Buchanan

had fought his way up the London literary ladder by dogged determination since his arrival in the metropolis in May, 1860. He eked out an uncertain living by writing poems, articles, and reviews for the *Athenaeum, Good Words,* and *Temple Bar.* In 1863, Moxon's published his first volume of poetry, *Undertones;* and, in 1865, Alexander Strahan brought out his second, *Idylls and Legends of Inverburn,* a book of poems dealing mostly with humble Scottish fisher folk. In the spring of 1866 he readied his third and most successful volume of poems, *London Poems,* for the press, and then moved himself and his family to the Scottish resort town of Oban for rest and recuperation.

We wonder why Payne had the poor judgment to take the Keats from Buchanan, who had apparently filled his part of the bargain, and give it to Swinburne. Payne obviously had little respect for a contract of any kind, as his later violation of contract in the case of Swinburne's *Poems and Ballads* shows. From what we know of the affair of the edition of Keats, Payne's conduct was highly unethical.

The next item in the quarrel is Buchanan's review of *Poems and Ballads* in the *Athenaeum* for August 4, 1866. The patronizing tone and the implication of Swinburne's homosexuality, along with the advice that he put behind him his evil advisers, show that Buchanan had accurate knowledge of Swinburne's private life and was using it to pay off an old score. Although Buchanan admitted in later years that he had been unfair in comparing Swinburne to Gito,[3] in 1866 he had no such compunction; for in September he published pseudonymously in the *Spectator* his mocking poem "The Session of the Poets," apparently based upon a gathering Moxon's had had for its authors on or about December 13, 1865. At that affair Swinburne's conduct had been so obnoxious that Lord Houghton, also present, later took him to task for being drunk and for insulting Tennyson.[4] In the poem, written cleverly in Swinburne's favorite anapests, Swinburne leaps to his feet at the dinner hour, and shocks the company with his wild talk:

> Up jumped, with his neck stretching out like a gander,
>   Master Swinburne, and squeal'd, glaring out thro' his hair,
> "All Virtue is bosh! Hallelujah for Landor!
> I disbelieve wholly in everything!—There!" [5]

So great is the consternation of the others that Tennyson, red with embarrassment, leaps to his feet, pounds the table with his fist, and commands: "To the door with the boy! Call a cab! He is tipsy!" and Swinburne is carried out.

Presumably, Buchanan, also one of Moxon's authors, was at the dinner, witnessed the same scene Lord Houghton complained of, and reported the details with basic accuracy; but he also used enough exaggeration and caricature to make the chief actor more ridiculous. Some time later Swinburne learned that Buchanan had authored the *Athenaeum* review, probably through his friend Joseph Knight, also on the staff of the *Athenaeum*. But to crack the inner councils of the *Spectator* to learn who had written the "Sessions" was much more difficult because of Editor Hutton's continuing animosity to his former reviewer. Dante Rossetti's letters show that he knew by the end of December, 1871, that the "Sessions" was Buchanan's, so it is safe to assume that Swinburne and William also knew it at that time. How much earlier they may have been aware of it, we do not know.

Swinburne hardly knew Buchanan as his assailant in the poem, but he may have been informed of him as the *Athenaeum* reviewer when he wrote his *Notes*. The tone of the *Notes* is, for him, quite mild. In the midst of some satirical remarks about the current popularity of idyls in poetry, he permitted himself a sneer at the Scotsman's expense: "If the Muse of the minute will not feast with 'gig-men' and their wives, she must mourn with costermongers and their trulls." [6] In a later essay Buchanan referred to "a gifted young contemporary, who . . . upbraids me for writing 'Idyls of the gallows and the gutter,' and singing songs of 'costermongers and their trulls.' " [7] Swinburne admitted in *Under the Microscope* that the reference was to him.[8]

Much more truculent was William Rossetti's attitude in his *Swinburne's Poems and Ballads*, published, according to the *Publishers' Circular*, between November 15-30, 1866, a week or two later than Swinburne's *Notes*, and at the same time as the republication of *Poems and Ballads*. William opens his essay with a vicious slash at the reviewer-poet: "The advent of a new great poet is sure to cause a commotion of one kind or another; and it would be hard were this otherwise in times like ours, when the advent of even so poor and pretentious a poetaster as a Robert Buchanan stirs storms in teapots." [9]

In the *Memoir* of his brother, William said he wrote this insult because he already knew of Buchanan's attack on Swinburne; but, if so, it was the review, not the poem, because we have no letters from him informing Swinburne, still at "Holmwood" on November 12, about who wrote the "Session." [10] However, when Buchanan published his joshing riposte to Swinburne's *Notes* in the *Athenaeum* of November 3, 1866,[11] Swinburne's letter to William Rossetti on November 12 revealed that he knew Buchanan had written it, but that he had taken no great offense.[12] His mood was still somewhat mild when he published his article "Mr. Arnold's New Poems" in the *Fortnightly Review* in October, 1867, because he contented himself with a slightly disparaging reference to David Gray, a dead Scottish poet and former close friend of Buchanan and a protégé of Lord Houghton. In connection with his disapproval of Wordsworth's doctrine that, if a poet were inspired he did not need to master the technique of his craft, Swinburne remarked: "Such talk as this of Wordsworth's is the poison of poor souls like David Gray." [13] When Swinburne published this essay in *Essays and Studies* (1875), he added a lengthy footnote attacking Gray with the utmost scorn and ill feeling.[14] Buchanan later cited this footnote as his reason for attacking Dante Rossetti and Swinburne in his "The Fleshly School of Poetry" of 1871, but he is in error. The note was not printed until after the attack.

Indeed the feeling between Buchanan and Swinburne in 1867-1869 amounted to little more than aversion. On January 26, 1869, Swinburne wrote Buchanan a courteous note regretting his inability to attend the Scotsman's public reading of his poems in London on the previous day because the invitation and complimentary ticket Buchanan had sent had arrived too late.[15] The tone of the letter is formal, but civil and also somewhat complimentary since Swinburne expresses his regret at missing the pleasure of hearing Buchanan read.

In 1868 Buchanan published his *David Gray and Other Essays* with the reference to the "gifted young contemporary" we have already noted, and in January, 1870, he evened his score with William Rossetti with a harsh review in the *Athenaeum* of his edition of Shelley. Buchanan stated that Rossetti had mistaken his vocation because he lacked sufficient material, critical insight, and the good taste necessary to an editor of such a project.[16]

Then came the climax in which Dante Gabriel Rossetti, who had buried his manuscript volume of poems in the coffin of Elizabeth Siddal Rossetti in 1862 as an act of penance, allowed himself to be persuaded by the scapegrace Charles Augustus Howell to exhume and publish them. The exhumation took place in the fall of 1869 without Rossetti's informing his family or Swinburne until it was done. Swinburne assisted Rossetti in readying the volume for the press, and it came out in the latter part of April, 1870, containing not only the exhumed poems but many others Rossetti had written in the intervening years. Several of the additions, as Oswald Doughty shows in his biography of Rossetti, dealt with his singular affair with Mrs. Jane Morris wife of William Morris, especially many of the "House of Life" sonnets.

Rossetti was not unmindful of what had happened to Swinburne's *Poems and Ballads*, nor was he unaware that several of the poems in his own volume were so frank in their expression of sexual passion and desire as to violate Victorian standards of morality. Moreover, he had a psychotic fear of adverse criticism. Therefore he "worked the oracle," as the phrase was, by arranging ahead of time that his book would be reviewed in most of the leading reviews by his friends. When the *Poems* came out, it met with a chorus of praise with, here and there, a few off-key notes from the magazines he had been unable to reach.

Two factors need to be taken into account here. Since 1868, Rossetti had been showing signs of the same mental trouble that had plagued his father's last years—increasing melancholy, a persecution complex coupled with suspicion of others, and a growing tendency to hallucinations. His Bohemian life, with its irregular hours, use of alcohol, and sexual excesses, only hastened the schizophrenia that unmistakably afflicted him; and when, in 1869 or 1870, he began to use chloral in increasing doses to overcome insomnia, he was indeed in a bad way.

The other factor is that at least since Swinburne's debacle in 1866, word had been getting about literary London that

Rossetti's influence was chiefly responsible. Such exhibitions as the one told by Sir William Hardman of Swinburne extolling de Sade at Rossetti's smoker helped create the impression.[17] Gossip of Rossetti's philanderings at his studio with a veritable procession of women from Jane Morris to Fanny Cornforth intensified it. In the view of many he was an evil Italian Svengali who had hypnotized and vitiated a promising young English poet of noble lineage. Something should be done about it.

While the furor about *Poems and Ballads* was at its height, Tennyson remarked publicly that Rossetti and possibly Lord Houghton were responsible for encouraging Swinburne in this direction. On October 6, 1866, Rossetti wrote Tennyson a letter denying the charge and claiming that he had struggled against this tendency in Swinburne.[18] As we know, his statement is untrue. By precept and example he had contributed materially to the worsening of Swinburne's character. Nor is it likely that Tennyson was befooled by Rossetti's disavowal. Ruskin knew most of the details of Rossetti's unsavory life and character, and he was in a position to gauge accurately his effect upon Swinburne. Ruskin met frequently and talked with Tennyson, Browning, Jowett, and other leading men of the time. It is reasonable to assume that he told them what he knew of the case and that they believed him rather than Rossetti.

Rossetti's reputation suffered also from the fact that though Swinburne's verse took a new direction in March, 1867, the downhill trend of his personal life continued and even accelerated in the years from 1866 to 1871. His alcholism and abnormal sexual excesses increased to such a degree that the trips of his father to London to take him home for rest and medical treatment became more and more frequent. Mazzini felt certain that Swinburne's death was imminent and grew impatient for the Italian songs to be published before it was too late.

His condition was dramatized and advertised by several events of a public character. His excesses increased his susceptibility to a form of epilepsy which manifested itself in fainting fits. In, July 1867, he toppled over at one of Lord Houghton's breakfasts; in October, he cut his face in what he described as a fall from a hansom which could have been caused by another fit. In 1867 and 1868 he had a well publicized affair with the notorious Adah Isaacs Menken, an American equestrienne who rode a horse bareback around the stage in a dramatization of Byron's *Mazeppa*. Like Chaucer's Wife of Bath, she had been married five times and had had many affairs, the best known being with the elder Alexander Dumas and with Swinburne. Swinburne apparently enjoyed the affair and even permitted pictures of Adah Menken and himself together to be posted in shop windows around London, possibly with the notion of offsetting rumors of his homosexuality. The casual fashion in which he tells George Powell of her death in Paris in August, 1868, shows how little she meant to him.

The fainting fits continued. On July 10, 1868, he blacked out in the British Museum, cut his forehead in a fall, and was carried out unconscious. The event appeared in the papers with such pessimistic accounts of his health that Jowett wrote him a friendly letter advising him to mend his ways and offering him money if he needed it. Swinburne, struck with this kindness from an unexpected source, immediately wrote his gratitude to his old master. From this time his friendship with Jowett grew until the scholar's death in 1893, and it led to vacation trips together. The probability is that Jowett's reentry into his life was no accident, but was only one result of a widespread anxiety about Swinburne and a determination to save him from the baneful influences into which he had fallen in London. I suspect Ruskin as the intermediary, maybe at the request of the Admiral or Lady Jane.

The sensational publicity continued when Swinburne was nearly drowned at Étretat on the French coast in October, 1868, while vacationing with the sinister George Powell. Caught by an undertow, he was carried out to sea and would surely have been drowned but for the timely arrival of a French fishing boat.

Swinburne's publication in 1868 of the *Blake* and "Ave Atque Vale," the poetic obituary to Baudelaire, both of which had been written when he had been under the influence of "art for art's sake," only confirmed the public impression that he was still devoted to the aesthetic ideals of *Poems and Ballads*. Moreover, his "Notes on Some Pictures of 1868" paid glowing tributes to several of Rossetti's pictures: "the sweet luxurious mouth" of "Lilith," expressive of "the warm repose of passion sure of its delight"; the "glorious bosom" of the "Venus Verticordia"; and the praise of both Whistler and Rossetti for their devotion to beauty.[19] All these stray bits of evidence could be linked together in a cause and effect relationship indicting Rossetti for a major share in the corruption of Swinburne.

The final touch to Rossetti's image as Swinburne's seducer was provided by Swinburne's ecstatic review of Rossetti's *Poems* in the *Fortnightly Review* in May, 1870. John Morley, author of the *Saturday Review* blast at *Poems and Ballads* in 1866, had become editor of the *Fortnightly* in 1867. Swinburne had been introduced to him by Joseph Knight, a friend of both, and the two had become such good friends that Swinburne became a regular contributor to the *Fortnightly*. Morley never summoned sufficient courage to tell Swinburne that he had written the review, nor did Swinburne ever tell Morley that he knew he had written it; however, they got along so well that, when Swinburne asked Morley's permission to review Rossetti's book, it was given at once.

"It is my devout intention to cut it fat. . . ." Swinburne wrote Dante Rossetti on February 24, 1870, using a butcher's terminology for cutting meat with plenty of suet to describe his review of Rossetti's book.[20] He cut it too fat and did Rossetti more harm than good. The review runs to about fifteen thousand words, a staggering total even for those days. It is a continuous panegyric in lyrical prose with showers of adjectives and extravagant claims. Rossetti is compared not unfavorably with Shakespeare as a sonneteer. No English poet of the day stands higher and few as high—Tennyson, Browning, and Arnold, possibly. Two-thirds of the way through the review he proudly acknowledges Rossetti to be ". . . the great artist by the light of whose genius and kindly guidance he [Morris] put forth the first fruits of his work, as I did afterwards." [21]

To shield Rossetti from the charges of paganism fastened upon *Poems and Ballads,* Swinburne claims that much of Rossetti's verse is Christian and even Catholic, but of a sincere kind, much superior to that of Browning or Newman. Unfortunately, when he gets down to particulars, he forgets this claim; reveling in the sensuous qualities of Rossetti's verse, he describes it as "fleshly." Of the "House of Life" sonnets: "No nakedness could be more harmonious, more consummate in its fleshly sculpture, than the imperial array and ornament of this august poetry." [22] Of the "Songs" following the "House of Life": "In all the glorious poem built up of all these poems there is no great quality more notable than the sweet and sovereign unity of perfect spirit and sense, of fleshly form and intellectual fire." [23] The poem "Lilith," written for Rossetti's picture, makes the reader "feel face to face the very vision of the old tale, and no symbol or shadow, but a bodily shape and a fleshly charm, dominant in ear and eye." [24]

Still in Scotland during 1870-1871 and in ill health, Buchanan did not get around to attacking Rossetti and Swinburne till eighteen months after the publication of *Poems*. In the *Contemporary Review* for October, 1871, appeared his "The Fleshly School of Poetry: Mr. D. G. Rossetti," filling some seventeen pages of that journal. He is unquestionably following the lead of James Russell Lowell in his review of Rossetti's *Poems* in the *North American Review* for October, 1870, six months after the publication of the book and *one year* before the appearance of Buchanan's article. Buchanan, in fact, quotes Lowell in the final paragraph of his article, prefacing the quotation with the remark that he agrees "substantially" with the opinion of the reviewer.

Lowell's article is truly great criticism. The public, he says, is skeptical of the claims of Swinburne, Morris, and William Rossetti that Dante Rossetti is a great poet, because he has hitherto refused to publish and because they were known to be close to him and not reliable judges in such matters. Rossetti he thinks a second rate poet because ". . . he is all feelings and desires . . ." but ". . . of thought and imagination he has next to nothing." [25] He is self-centered, is fond of clothing himself in a false medieval garb, and refuses to deal with contemporary life. Lowell finds a note of morbid eroticism in many of the poems, especially in "Jenny," and he accuses Rossetti of using "a set of properties" to delude the unsuspecting reader.[26] The love which Rossetti deals with is "a sensuous and sexual love, refined to some extent by that sort of worship of one's mistress as saint and divinity which the early Italians made a fashion, certainly, whether or not it was ever a faith by which they lived." [27] Lowell's final opinion is that Rossetti's eventual poetic rating will fall much below what his friends have claimed and that the world will consider him to be ". . . a man of the temperament of genius lacking power to give effect, in words at least, to a nature and gifts rare rather than strong or valuable, nevertheless it will be admitted that he is an elaborately skilful love-poet of narrow range who affords an occasional touch that makes the reader hesitate and consider whether he has not now and again struggled out and really emerged as a poet worthy of the name." [28]

Buchanan obviously had Swinburne's and Lowell's reviews before him when he wrote his article. Like Lowell, he minimizes Rossetti's importance, saying that in a cast of *Hamlet* he would play Osric to Tennyson's and Browning's Hamlet, and he accuses Rossetti, Morris, and Swinburne of having formed a "Mutual Admiration School" to praise each other's works. He quotes from Morris's and Swinburne's reviews to prove his point. Like Lowell, too, he finds Rossetti's chief fault to be sexuality disguised as love, his emphasis centering upon the sonnet "Nuptial Sleep," quoted in full. And he agrees with Lowell that the disguise for the persistent strain of lust is a "grotesque mediaevalism," imitated from Dante, though the style is taken from Tennyson, Browning, and Mrs. Browning. With evident gusto he takes both Rossetti and Swinburne to task for having their lovers of both sexes "bite, scratch, scream, bubble, munch, sweat, writhe, twist, wriggle, foam" in their lovemaking.[29] His opinion coincides with Lowell's that Rossetti's verse has infrequent passages of real beauty, but such passages are marred by the recurrent note of illicit sexuality. Like Lowell also, he accuses Rossetti of being completely absorbed in himself and his emotions. But he goes beyond the American critic in two notable particulars: He objects to the heartlessness of the monologuist in "Jenny" and to the irregularity of rhythm which forces the reader to put the accent on the wrong syllable in such words as "Haymar*ket*" and "li*ly*."

From Swinburne's review he took the word "fleshly" and flung it like a stone at Rossetti, using it as the key word of his title as well. The phrase Swinburne employs to praise Rossetti's diction, "the golden affluence of words," recurs mockingly throughout the review. And Swinburne comes in for minor attention as one who has recently written several novels, the statement being followed by an exclamation point in parentheses, manifestly an oblique reference to the content of *Lesbia Brandon* and of *A Year's Letters*. In the *Hamlet* cast Buchanan has Swinburne and Morris in the unflattering roles of Rosencrantz and Guildenstern; as a poet Swinburne is "transcendently superficial"; in *Poems and*

Ballads he is "only a little mad boy letting off squibs; not a great strong man, who might be really dangerous to society," and his review of *Poems* is "a hysteria of admiration." [30]

Buchanan knew the fury his review would raise, so he took pains to avert suspicion by scattering a few false leads through it. He includes himself as Cornelius in the *Hamlet,* whereas anyone knowing him would suppose that his vanity would have had him at least as Horatio; and he speaks of himself as having been accused of "maudlin sentiment and affected tenderness" in his "quasi-lyrical" poems.[31] The review was signed "Thomas Maitland."

The dodge worked well for a time. However, even as early as mid-October Rossetti heard rumors that Buchanan was the author, and by December he was fairly certain.[32] An insulting article in the *Athenaeum* for December 9, 1871, by Sidney Colvin brought an angry admission from Buchanan and a denial from Publisher Strahan. Buchanan's letter was dated from London, but he had apparently replied in such hot haste that he and Strahan had been unable to work out a unified strategy, and their contradictory letters to the *Athenaeum* were the embarrassing result.

Quick to capitalize on the windfall, the *Athenaeum* printed both letters on December 16, adding the caustic comment that Buchanan's was "an edifying comment" on Strahan's and that Buchanan should have signed his own name to the article and not have delayed his admission until he had been found out. The implication of the comment is that Buchanan and Strahan are liars tripped up by their own falsehoods.

Buchanan's letter denied that he had had anything to do with the addition of the pseudonym or with the "suppression" of his name, and promised that he would reissue the article "with many additions," under his own name, and published by Strahan. He added that "The grave responsibility of not agreeing with Mr. Rossetti's friends . . . will thus be transferred . . . to my own shoulders." [33]

The same issue of the *Athenaeum* carrying the fiasco of the letters had a two-thousand-word defense of his *Poems* by Rossetti. Writing it in the form of a letter also and titling it "The Stealthy School of Criticism," Rossetti denies the charge of sensuality, and countercharges that Buchanan has quoted him out of

context and distorted his meaning. On the question of the sensuality of "Nuptial Sleep," he dodges the issue by asserting that it
is not a whole poem, but only one item in a cycle of sonnets; that
it should be considered only in the context of the cycle, and
that on no ground should it be taken as his own view of love.[34]
(Basically, this last is the same argument Swinburne used in his
defense of *Poems and Ballads*.) In proof of his assertion Rossetti
quotes in full his sonnet "Love-Sweetness" and adds: "Any reader
may bring any artistic charge he pleases against the above
sonnet; but one charge it would be impossible to maintain against
the writer of the series in which it occurs, and that is, the wish on
his part to assert that the body is greater than the soul." [35]

Now the sonnet in question has a quite sensuous description
of a voluptuous lady, her hair loosened and falling about the
lover's face, and his kissing of her cheeks, neck, and eyelids in
the first eight lines; the last six voice the sentiment that without
the fervor of her heart and "the swift beat/ And soft subsidence
of the spirit's wing" all her physical attractions "would lose their
sweet. . . ." [36]

This sonnet does not stultify the charge of sensuality against
Rossetti—not at all. But he claims that it does. And this is his
method throughout the defense: first, state the charge; second,
give a quotation from the *Poems*; third, assert that he has dis-
proved the charge. After much lengthy quotation, he closes by
remonstrating against the use of the pseudonym by one
poet attacking another. Rossetti asserts piously that, for justice,
he would leave Buchanan to his conscience, for he was obviously
disturbed or he would not have used the pseudonym in the first
place (a clever way of branding as a lie Buchanan's denial that
he had affixed the pseudonym). He then remarks caustically that
this was the very man who "from behind his mask" had accused
him of insincerity.[37]

Rossetti's protestations of the innocence of his "House of Life"
sonnets and of his intentions in them acquire a hollow sound and
a touch of Voltairean irony from the fact that when Buchanan's
Fleshly article appeared in October, 1871, Rossetti was just completing three months of cohabitation at "Kelmscott Manor" with
Mrs. Jane Morris, to whom, we now know, many of the sonnets
were written. Husband William Morris had the curious notion
that if he could not hold his wife's love, he had no right to inter-

fere with her transferring it to another man. With full knowledge that Rossetti was with his wife, Morris remained away for most of the time.[38]

We wonder how Rossetti could have had the effrontery to accuse Buchanan of insincerity and of not telling the truth. Yet it must be admitted that repetition of the accusation of falsehood, as well as the suggestion of treason in one poet's attacking another, was clever. It kept Buchanan where the *Athenaeum* had put him when it printed his and Strahan's letters—squarely on the defensive; and it dragged a red herring across the trail to divert him and the public from the main question of the morality or immorality of Rossetti's poems. Buchanan attempted to revive the central issue with his booklet *The Fleshly School of Poetry and Other Phenomena of the Day,* published by Strahan in the first week of May, 1872. But instead of helping matters, he played into the hands of his foes by going to such ridiculous lengths in his pursuit of fleshliness that he completely stultified both himself and his case. Everywhere he goes in London, he says, he sees evidence of the growing menace of fleshliness: on drawingroom tables, in poems read by girls, in confectionery stores with "models of the female Leg, the whole definite and elegant article as far as the thigh, with a fringe of paper cut in imitation of the female drawers and embroidered in the female fashion!" [39]

While all this controversy was going on, Swinburne was having his troubles. His dissipations were increasing, and the periods of time he was able to be in London before his health broke down and he had to be taken to "Holmwood" for care grew ever shorter. In London early in 1871 he soon got into such a condition that, his father being ill, his parents had to enlist Rossetti's aid in getting him to "Holmwood." They kept him there until August, when he took a vacation trip to Scotland with Jowett which lasted into mid-September. Then back to London, he was in such bad shape in early October that the Admiral came, closed out his tenancy of his apartment, moved his goods into storage, and took him home, apparently intending that he should not return.

On February 11, 1871, his worried mother wrote Rossetti a most revealing letter with clear implications that she and the Admiral well knew the exact cause of his trouble. Above all, she says, they wish he would stay away from London and remain at "Holmwood"; and they have urged him to have his books and other necessaries brought there. Then she adds: "I fear his having his books would not keep him here—it is impossible but a mind like his should require the society of persons with minds and pursuits similar to his own, unless he could make up his mind to remain here as a means of conquering his fearful propensity—for a time he is perfectly happy and his health as good as possible, he says how much better he can work here and how much better he feels." [40] But their only way of keeping him there against his will was to go to court, prove him mentally incompetent, and have him committed either to an institution or to their care. This they were not willing to do—yet.

While at "Holmwood," he received a letter early in November, 1871, from Frederick Locker with the news that Buchanan was the author of the *Contemporary* article. On November 13 he passed the word along to Rossetti, urging him to write and publish a reply. Either he was not satisfied with Rossetti's defense, or Buchanan's threat to expand his article into a booklet prodded him into action. He had also learned by this time of Buchanan's authorship of "The Session." At any rate he set about his own reply in *Under the Microscope,* and it appeared in the bookstalls by early July, 1872.

Swinburne begins by explaining that since it is a scientific age, he plans to spend an hour in scientific research and to set forth his findings in this book. The two "bugs" he examines are Alfred Austin—whose *Poetry of the Period* contains some caustic strictures on Swinburne—and Robert Buchanan. The first half of the essay deals with Austin by way of warm-up for the main bout with Buchanan. Swinburne does not argue with Buchanan, as Rossetti makes a show of doing in "The Stealthy School"; he belabors him with epithets, insults, and scurrilous insinuations, leaving him not a shred of dignity as a human being, but casting him aside at the end as a foul serpent too loathsome to touch.

He begins by rating Buchanan as far below Austin as Austin is beneath Tennyson and Browning; and he insinuates that, like Petronius, the Scotsman is a homosexual. Noting the hope of some critics that Buchanan might develop into a major poet, Swinburne says positively: "The tadpole poet will never grow into anything bigger than a frog; not though in that stage of development he should puff and blow himself till he bursts with windy adulation at the heels of the laurelled ox." [41]

Raging in this vein through many pages of violent rhetoric, he gives free rein to the sadistic side of his nature and aptly illustrates his mother's later criticism of him that he never knew when to stop. His friends had often flattered him on his ability to annihilate with words; in the Fleshly article Buchanan had remarked on his genius for fashioning "alliterative thunderbolts." [42] Plainly Swinburne saw himself here as an angry schoolmaster cutting to bloody shreds the back and bottom of a vile boy. But he rages so long, so loud, and so uncontrollably that he is unconvincing. The Anglo-Saxon image of an angry man is of one who says only a few words but makes those few count because he is ready to back them up with action if necessary. In *Under the Microscope* Swinburne was demonstrating his lack of manly self-control.

This was precisely the weakness Buchanan played up in a squib called "The Monkey and the Microscope" he wrote by way of reply and published in *St. Paul's Magazine* for August, 1872:

> *A clever Monkey—he can squeak,*
> *Scream, bite, munch, mumble, all but speak;*
> *Studies not merely monkey-sport*
> *But vices of a human sort;*
> *Is petulant to most, but sweet*
> *To those who pat him, give him meat;*
> *Can imitate to admiration*
> *Man's gestures, gait, gesticulation;*
> *Is amorous, and takes no pain*
> *To hide his Aphrodital vein;*
> *And altogether, trimly drest*
> *In human breeches, coat, and vest,*
> *Looks human, and upon the whole*
> *Lacks nothing, save perchance a Soul.*[43]

The controversy lay dormant till 1875, when Swinburne published his *Essays and Studies,* including his "Matthew Arnold's New Poems" with the addition of the patronizing footnote on Gray we have discussed earlier. The note enraged Buchanan far more than *Under the Microscope.* He vowed revenge and waited his opportunity. It came in the summer of 1875 with the publication of an anonymous poem *Jonas Fisher,* really by James Carnegie, the Earl of Southesk, but with so many of the characteristics of Buchanan's verse—humanitarianism, anti-Catholicism, strictures on literary and artistic immorality—that Swinburne felt sure it was his. He was quick to retaliate with four lines of scornful verse to the *Examiner:*

> *EPITAPH ON A SLANDERER*
> *He whose heart and soul and tongue*
> *Once above-ground stunk and stung,*
> *Now less noisome than before,*
> *Stinks here still, but stings no more.*
> A. C. Swinburne.[44]

A week later the *Examiner* reviewed *Jonas Fisher,* devoting its first paragraph to a satirical speculation that Buchanan was the probable author. On December 4, Buchanan published in the *Athenaeum* a flat disavowal, and in the *Examiner* for December 11, Swinburne burlesqued the whole matter of the original Fleshly article and the pseudonym and the pseudonymous *Jonas Fisher* with a letter titled "The Devil's Due" and signed "Thomas Maitland." The letter opens with a long paragraph imitating the style of Buchanan's critical essays with a bewildering number of reservations, insinuations, and definitions. Then it turns to the question of authorship and observes that *Jonas Fisher* could as well be attributed to Satan as to "the polypseudonymous lyrist and libeller in question." [45]

However, Swinburne continues, the author does not seem to be Buchanan because he has not learned to praise his own works and throw dirt on the works of others. Moreover, *Jonas* is in the style of the "Bab Ballads," a style not yet mastered by Buchanan. Here he adds a lengthy note instructing his publisher to add still another note, heavily satirizing all of Buchanan's and Strahan's notes to the *Athenaeum:*

The writer of the above being at present away from London, on a cruise among the Philippine Islands, in his steam yacht (the *Skulk,* Captain Shuffleton master), is, as can be proved on the oath or the solemn word of honour of the editor, publisher, and proprietor, respon-

sible neither for an article which might with equal foundation be attributed to Cardinal Manning, or to Mr. Gladstone, or any other writer
in the *Contemporary Review,* as to its actual author; nor for the adop-
tion of a signature under which his friends in general . . . have
thought it best and wisest to shelter his personal responsibility from
any chance of attack.[46]

II *The Trial*

This time Swinburne had gone too far, and Buchanan had him
at last on a charge of libel. The trial took place in London on
June 29, 30, and July 1, 1876. Buchanan sued P. A. Taylor, owner
of the *Examiner,* for £5,000 for libel. At the outset, Taylor's lawyers attempted to have the suit transferred to Swinburne; but
MacClymont, one of Buchanan's lawyers, was a friend of John
Nichol, who successfully interceded with him to have the suit remain against Taylor. Buchanan's Fleshly School article and book
were brought into the case, as were "The Session of the Poets" and
his essay praising Whitman. Buchanan unblushingly insisted
that his remarks in the poem were against Swinburne's writings,
not his person. When a book of Whitman's poems was submitted to the judge and the jury for silent examination because
they were too evil to be read aloud, the Scotsman replied that he
had not condemned Whitman as he had the Fleshly writers because he considered the American fundamentally "a spiritual person." [47]

Swinburne did not escape unscathed. When Justice Archibald
demanded the reason Buchanan's attorneys had sued Taylor instead of Swinburne, they answered that the poet was a "man of
straw" who had not the money to pay the damages, so they had
taken Taylor instead. Likewise when several of Swinburne's and
Rossetti's poems were read, Archibald said the world would have
been better off if they had never been written.

In his summation to the jury, Justice Archibald indicated quite
clearly that he favored the defendant, but the jury took only
twenty minutes to bring in a verdict of £150 for Buchanan,
hardly enough to pay his attorneys' fees. Watts-Dunton, who
acted as Swinburne's adviser, tried to persuade him to pay
part or all of the damages, perhaps on the ground that William
Minto, editor of the *Examiner,* had not realized the libelous nature of Swinburne's satirical letters because he had not been fa-

miliar with the background of the Fleshly Controversy, whereas Swinburne did know their full import. Swinburne refused.

For him the trial had been a dreadful ordeal that scarred his soul. He had been taught a lesson that he never forgot. His proud name had been dragged into court and made ridiculous; his poems had been read aloud in public and scoffed at; he had been scorned as an ineffectual creature too mean to prosecute.

For Swinburne the Fleshly Controversy was at an end. Not one word more did he publish about Buchanan. But, as his letters show, his hatred continued to burn fiercely until his death in 1909.

CHAPTER 8

The Recluse of Putney

AS STATED in the preface, the purpose of this book is to render Swinburne's work understandable to the modern reader. For him, more than for most men of letters, the achievement of such an aim necessitates an examination of the various aesthetic and philosophical influences affecting him and leaving their impress upon his writings. We have followed him through such stages as classicism, republicanism, Pre-Raphaelitism, Baudelaireism, and Positivism. In all of these he was, of course, dominated by others whose personalities captured his fancy. Their ideas became so completely and implicitly his that he accepted them in most cases without apparent reservation or question. And, since he wrote as he thought, we can readily follow the parade of ideas in his works.

He was to undergo one final transformation in his life and thought, a transformation so comprehensive, so far-reaching in its consequences, that it must be taken into consideration in discussing the works of the latter half of his life. Unlike the other stages in his career, this one has no convenient label. It is a period of growing conservatism, of increasing patriotism, of angry repudiation of some of his earlier enthusiasms, and, finally, of lessening interest in the world about him.

The proclamation of the French Republic in 1870, the completion of Italian unification in the same year, the deaths of Mazzini in 1872 and of Napoleon III in 1873, left Swinburne without a cause to serve, a leader to follow, or a political tyrant to denounce. He was even more left high and dry when William Rossetti wrote him early in July, 1872, that Dante's condition was so bad that Swinburne should on no account try to see him. Even though Dante recovered and went about almost as usual, their friendship was completely at an end; the two men never thereafter met nor had any kind of correspondence with each other. Swinburne was hurt and bewildered by such conduct on the part of his old friend, and he remained in the dark as to the reason for it. And, although he and William remained as close friends as ever, William never threw any light on the matter.

But, as we have shown, the answer may well lie in the fact that Dante and William concluded that Buchanan's attack on Dante had come about because of the widespread suspicion that Dante had corrupted Swinburne and seduced him into evil paths. The best preventive for such attacks in future, therefore, was the complete severance of all relations between Rossetti and his erstwhile disciple.

From 1872 to 1877 a number of factors contributed to keeping Swinburne at "Holmwood" and out of the dangerous environment of London. As his dissipations increased, the periods of time he could be in London before it became necessary for his father or someone else to take him to "Holmwood" for recuperation grew progressively shorter. Likewise he was short of money because Hotten, with whom his difficulties had been mounting, paid him very little; also, as a necessary measure toward keeping him out of the metropolis, Swinburne's father may have either curtailed or discontinued altogether the allowance of £200 he had been paying him since 1861. Under the circumstances who could blame him?

Furthermore, Swinburne was both shocked and frightened in 1873 when scandalous rumors of abnormal sexual practices attached themselves to Simeon Solomon's name and circulated widely throughout London. No man who cared for his own good name, he wrote Watts, could afford to have anything to do with such a person. But for the past ten years or more he had had only too much to do with Solomon, publicly and privately, having gone so far as to publish an article on the young painter's poems in *The Dark Blue* in July, 1871.[1] Better, then, to stay out of London while the wave of scandal was at the crest.

Another quieting influence had entered actively into Swinburne's life in 1872 in Walter Theodore Watts (later Watts-Dunton). A country solicitor who yearned for a literary career, he took up residence in London and made himself extremely useful to both Dante Rossetti and Swinburne in handling and straightening out their tangled financial affairs. He took over negotiations with the slippery Hotten, and he had already instituted legal action to force him to settle with Swinburne when the publisher died suddenly in June, 1873. Thereupon Watts effected a much more amicable and profitable arrangement with Andrew Chatto, Hotten's reputable successor, who became henceforth Swinburne's publisher. From this time on, Watts exerted a steady, subtle influence to bring Swinburne back into the paths of respectability and to rule out of his life anything of a disturbing or unsettling nature. For the rest of Swinburne's life, Watts served without pay as his literary agent, shrewdly marketing his wares for the best possible prices.

After the Fleshly School trial of 1876, in which Watts again acted as Swinburne's adviser, the poet returned to "Holmwood" until the death of Admiral Swinburne at the age of eighty on March 5, 1877, brought him back to London with his inheritance of £5,000 at his disposal. As might be expected, he returned with such a will to his old life of dissipation and excess that on May 31, 1878, he was too ill to accept Hugo's invitation to be his guest at the festival in honor of Voltaire. Swinburne's landlady at Great James Street, Mrs. Jane Magill, kept Lady Jane informed of what was going on. Lord Houghton, who visited him in July, 1878, found him in such dire straits that he wrote Lady Jane recommending medical supervision, but she answered helplessly that she had no power to enforce it. Instead, she wrote Watts, who lived only a few doors away from Swinburne's apartment, to investigate and report to her.[2]

Finally, in June, 1879, Watts carried Swinburne from his rooms in what biographers agree was a nearly dying condition, and, in due course, moved him to "The Pines" at Putney, a suburb of London, where they took a house together and continued to live until Swinburne's death in 1909. Under Watts' watchful eye and gentle but determined persuasion, the poet was weaned away from alcohol and guided into a regular and progressively reclusive existence. More and more he came to rely upon Watts and to defer to his judgment until it finally became almost impossible to see Swinburne without first securing Watts' permission.

To say, as some biographers do, that Swinburne became little more than Watts' puppet and that his writings during these final years were, to use Shakespeare's phrase in *Hamlet*, "weary, stale, flat, and unprofitable," is not to state the whole truth. Undoubtedly, Watts's influence was pronounced, as was that of the other older men whom Swinburne trusted and admired; but it was not absolute. On some notable occasions Swinburne overruled Watts, as he did in October, 1882, to drag him to Paris for the fiftieth anniversary of Hugo's *Le Roi s'Amuse.* Generally, the two got along very well and grew gracefully old in the quiet repose of "The Pines." Swinburne became noticeably more conservative and much more of an English patriot instead of an objector to English complacency, even going so far as to praise Queen Victoria in his poem "Euonymos" for her courage in the assassination attempt of 1882. His conservatism is also apparent in his disavowal of "art for art's sake" in the essay "Mr. Whistler's Lecture on Art" of 1887 and in "The Armada," the tricentennial poem of 1888 hailing England as the "Mother more beloved than all who bear not all their children free." [3]

But to say that all this was solely the result of Watts's influence is going to an unwarranted extreme. In great part, I believe, it was the manifestation of the natural conservatism that comes with age, as well as the natural tendency, now that his father was dead and the antagonism between them ended, to adopt more and more the father's conservative viewpoint and outlook. For, like many other men, Swinburne, as he grew older, developed an understanding and appreciation of his father that he had been incapable of during the Admiral's lifetime.

Much has been made of the many poems Swinburne wrote after 1879 to Bertie Mason, Watts-Dunton's five-year-old nephew and the son of his sister, who lived close by. Generally, it has been cited as an evidence of the childish and rather spiritless personality that Swinburne is supposed to have become under the domination of Watts-Dunton. I can find no conclusive evidence that Swinburne developed such a personality, but I am willing to admit that he did lean heavily upon Watts-Dunton. His great love for children is one of the interesting phenomena of these later years. Even Watts-Dunton and Lady Jane were uneasy about it, obviously fearful that it might be one more manifestation of Swinburne's abnormal tendencies. But his love was not just for Bertie; it was for any child he came across, even two little girls he met in one of his morning walks about Putney. His emotion, however, is all love and tenderness rather than the former psychotic gloating over the prospect of beating them until they bled. My conjecture is that his relationship with Bertie Mason was a vicarious fatherhood that opened the floodgates and let his love flow as it never had before—not even when he was paying court to Mary Gordon in 1863-1864.

The extent of his literary production from 1872 to 1909 is truly remarkable, approximately four times the volume of that for the period from 1856 to 1872. As before 1872, it lies in the areas of drama, poetry, and criticism. It includes some of his best work and some of his poorest. In drama it ranges from the high point of *Erechtheus* to the nadir of *The Duke of Gandia;* in poetry, from the supreme beauty of *Tristram of Lyonesse* to the greeting-card bathos of "Babyhood"; in criticism, from the noble "Recollections of Professor Jowett" to the ignoble and lamentable "The New Terror," in which he exhumed and belabored the corpse of William Bell Scott. Its subject matter is truly catholic. Much of it is of a memorial character, with poetic tributes to a great number of friends, associates, and prominent persons who preceded him in death. Generally speaking, we find the focus of his attention increasingly upon things British, with a corresponding decrease of emphasis on foreign subjects and topics. He hadn't forgotten to hate, as his fierce denunciations of Russia, Germany, the Pope and the Catholic Church, Carlyle, and Furnivall show quite clearly; nor how to love and admire, as is evidenced by his devoted tributes to Hugo, Shelley, Charlotte and Emily Bronte, Landor, Dickens, Coleridge, and Mazzini. Newly present in the poetry is an almost Wordsworthian love of nature, with especial emphasis upon the sea, and considerably lessened are any traces of the abnormal sexuality so prominent in the earlier works.

I   The Drama

We could wish that Swinburne had not wasted his time in attempting to write dramas. To begin with, he had no knowledge of dramatic technique or of the requirements of the drama. Like Browning, Tennyson, and most of the other Victorian poets who tried their hands at the drama, he labored under the Shakespeare-complex that all dramas must be in blank verse, in five acts, and in the heroic tone and pattern. With such handicaps, realism and immediacy were precluded and artificiality insured. Nor did he have any notion of a central theme or core of meaning around which to build his dramas. Therefore organization and proportion are woefully absent from Swinburne's attempts, and some grotesque malformations occur. Nor did he have any idea of the practical demands and limitations of the stage. What he needed to do was what Shakespeare, Eugene O'Neill, or any other who has successfully written for the stage has had to do— get a job with an acting troupe and master the lore of the stage in the only way it can be mastered, by practical experience. For Swinburne this was, of course, out of the question, and his dramas, except for occasional passages of good poetry and some plausible dialogue, are failures.

The first drama of this period, and one of the worst, is *Bothwell* (1874), a huge monstrosity running to five hundred and thirty pages in the Bonchurch Edition, about five times as long as the uncut *Hamlet*. Swinburne was obviously overawed by history, including much that should have been omitted. In spots the poetry is excellent, but it is lost in a futile cause. An excellent example of Swinburne's total lack of dramatic know-how occurs in Act III when, after Bothwell tells Queen Mary that the battle is lost because the troops have deserted and left them hopelessly outnumbered by the approaching enemy, she launches into a bitter speech of about four hundred words—and this with disaster upon them and the speediest kind of action necessary!

In *Erechtheus* (1876), he returned to the classical material that had served so well in *Atalanta*. This time the result was not so happy, possibly because he wrote under the influence of Jowett and gave more attention to the classical tone and style of his verse than to its music. Swinburne wrote it almost like a school exercise, with little of "the fever and the fret" of real life anywhere in evidence.

Mary Stuart (1881) ends the trilogy which begins with *Chastelard,* and is dedicated to Victor Hugo, as are the two earlier dramas dealing with the unfortunate Scottish queen. Only about a third as long as *Bothwell,* this play deals with the imprisonment and execution of Mary Stuart at the hands of Elizabeth. Once again, the characters are cardboard figures stiffly going through their assigned roles with very little action, external or internal; and, as usual in Swinburne's dramas, the plot has no suspense.

Marino Faliero (1885), a play patterned after Byron's tragedy of the same title, is the story of an old man with a young wife.

The play deals with an octogenarian who takes the law into his hands to avenge an insult to his honor and ends up being beheaded for treason to the state. Swinburne makes him into a precursor of Mazzini with republican ideals and hatred of the Catholic clergy. Some suspense is injected with the villain's vow to have revenge upon Marino, but the insult to Marino is so casually reported that the old man's resorting to treason to avenge it seems highly improbable.

Of the four remaining tragedies—*Locrine* (1887), *The Sisters* (1892), *Rosamund, Queen of the Lombards* (1899), and *The Duke of Gandia* (1908)—the most interesting is *The Sisters* because of the autobiographical material it contains. Swinburne casts himself as Reginald Clavering, a hero of the battle of Waterloo. Two of Reginald's cousins, Mabel and Anne Dilston, are in love with him. He chooses Mabel to be his bride; and then jealous Anne poisons the both of them. *The Duke of Gandia* is the most regrettable of all the plays and a "throwback" to *Chastelard* (1865) and the worst of *Poems and Ballads* (1866). Consisting of only four scenes, *The Duke* is a playlet dealing with Pope Alexander VI; his concubine Vannozza Catanei; and their three children, Francesco, Caesar, and Lucrezia Borgia. Francesco, the duke, is murdered by an assassin hired by Caesar, who makes it clear to their grieving father than Francesco's death was expedient and that it will not cause Caesar to lose any sleep. Replete with suggestions of incest, absolute immorality, and dealing with characters who are monsters, not humans, the play is the kind of thing Swinburne should neither have written nor published.

II *The Criticism*

In the field of criticism Swinburne's publications during his final period include *Essays and Studies* (1875), *George Chapman* (1875), the *Note on the Muscovite Crusade* (1876), *A Note on Charlotte Bronte* (1877), *A Study of Shakespeare* (1880), *Miscellanies* (1886), *A Study of Victor Hugo* (1886), *A Study of Ben Jonson* (1889), *Studies in Prose and Poetry* (1894), and *The Age of Shakespeare* (1908). Like the dramas, most of Swinburne's critical works were misspent efforts marred by extravagant praise or fierce blame, depending upon whether the subject met with his approval or censure. But, as always, he showed that "the pleasure of praising" could not be enjoyed without drawing those unfortunate comparisons at the expense of others of whom he did not approve. A good example of this unfortunate propensity is the *Note on Charlotte Bronte,* which could as well be titled "An Attack on George Eliot," for that is what it equally is. He designates Charlotte Bronte as "one of the greatest among women" and then adds that her works will be read "with reverence and admiration . . . when even *Daniel Deronda* has gone the way of all waxwork, when even Miss Broughton no longer cometh up as a flower, and even Mrs. Oliphant is at length cut down like the grass." [4] What better way to call forth the Erinyes in all their fury?

The voluminous works about Shakespeare and the other Elizabethan playwrights and about such figures as Hugo, Landor, Shelley, and Coleridge we may pass over hurriedly because they are paeans of praise and nothing more. The criticism of the dramatists is further nullified by the fact, well illustrated by Swinburne's own dramas, that he lacked sufficient knowledge of the drama to criticize it intelligently.

In writing about the novel, it is interesting to note that he fell into the usual Victorian error with regard to Emily Bronte's *Wuthering Heights,* failing to understand it as a prose poem of a love so great that it transcends the grave, and regretting its ferocity and violence. But he does insist that its "noble purity" will more than offset such faults. Dickens he hails as the supreme Victorian literary figure, with *Great Expectations* and *David Copperfield* as his greatest novels.

In "Whitmania" he can find little to praise in the American bard whom he had admired in his "art-for-art's-sake" days except his views of death, his abundant sympathies, and his usually good intentions. Otherwise, the American often mistakes rhetoric for song, and he is frequently guilty of treating sex in a very coarse fashion! Whether Swinburne realized how far he had departed from his "not-for-girls" argument in *Notes on Poems and Reviews* of 1866 is debatable.

The *Note of an English Republican on the Muscovite Crusade* is a determined attack on Gladstone and Carlyle for their support of Russia in her dispute with Turkey. Swinburne had been angered by a comment made by Carlyle in 1874 that Swinburne's poetry showed that he was standing in a cesspool up to his chin and also contributing to its contents. He evened the score now by taunting Carlyle for supporting Russia because she had kept in subjection the "anarchic populations" in her part of the world, and sneered that Carlyle had never spoken or written a word in support of Italian freedom.

Perhaps the most regrettable piece of all is the essay "The New Terror" (1892), his enraged response to what he thought were traitorous and envious remarks made about him by his dead friend William Bell Scott in his *Autobiographical Notes*. Because William Minto, former editor of the *Examiner* when Swinburne's libelous remarks had been published therein, was also editor of Scott's autobiography, he shared in the attack. Scott, said Swinburne, was an "unspeakable Caledonian" who was guilty of "malignant impertinence of senile invention." And Minto, by his folly in permitting such scurrilous remarks to appear in print, had only succeeded in "stripping and gibbeting" the dead author.[5] It was a deplorable affair altogether, and, as in the case of *The Duke of Gandia,* one regrets that he wrote what he did.

Quite otherwise is his noble testimonial to Jowett, perhaps the finest essay he ever wrote. The tone and style are dignified and wholly appropriate to the subject. He testifies to Jowett's courage, enthusiasm, and modesty, praising him for rarely letting pedagogical formality displace the *bonhomie* of the cheerful friend and companion. It is a touching tribute from a devoted pupil to a great teacher.

III   *The Poetry*

As always, Swinburne's best work in his final period was in his poetry. Although he was out of his proper metier in the drama and criticism, in poetry he was supremely at home. He might not have the patience, the analytical objectivity, the technical competence to construct a long drama or a major work of criticism; but he did possess the fire, the imagination, the supreme and intuitive genius with rhythm and rhyme to create good and often truly great poetry.

His production in the last period is truly remarkable. Beginning with *Songs of Two Nations* (1875), it includes *Poems and Ballads, Second Series* (1878), *Songs of the Springtides* (1880), *Studies in Song* (1880), *The Heptalogia* (1880), *Tristram of Lyonesse* (1882), *A Century of Roundels* (1883), *A Midsummer Holiday*

(1884), *Poems and Ballads, Third Series* (1889), *Astrophel and Other Poems* (1894), *The Tale of Balen* (1896), *Rosamund, Queen of the Lombards* (1899), and *A Channel Passage and Other Poems* (1904). In addition to these, many other poems, some of them written during his Oxford days, were posthumously published by the noted literary forger, Thomas J. Wise, to whom Watts-Dunton, Swinburne's sole heir, sold them following the poet's death.

Perhaps the best of these are the autobiographical poems "Thalassius" and "On the Cliffs," and a new rendering of the Tristram and Isolde story, entitled *Tristram of Lyonesse.* "Thalassius," literally "the sea-man" in Greek, tells the story of Swinburne's life in its relations to the sea. The child of Apollo and Cymothoe, the sun and the sea, Swinburne says he was found lying on the beach by one "born of man's most highest and heavenliest birth"—Landor—whose songs teach him to despise tyranny, to love liberty, and to aspire to sing songs "goldener than gold." The boy encounters love but learns bitterly that it is only death in disguise. Disillusioned, he turns to lust and dissipation only to learn that these make him feel unclean. He returns to the sea, which purges his soul and restores his faith so that he is enabled once again to sing his songs joyfully.

The setting of "On the Cliffs" is also by the sea, for Swinburne, standing at twilight on a cliff, looks out over the calm sea and meditates upon the great mysteries of life and death. This poem was written in July and August, 1879, while he was at "Holmwood," shortly after Watts-Dunton had saved him from certain death. His mood is therefore understandably pensive and introspective. Like Matthew Arnold in "Dover Beach," Swinburne stands apart and views himself, in relation to the rest of mankind and to the enigma of existence.

Nowhere else does he discuss the effect of his physical peculiarity upon his life and poetry with the frankness that is here. All pretense, all "front," all borrowed philosophies and enthusiasms, all the defenses that Swinburne's intrinsically shy spirit had erected between itself and the world are gone. He reveals his naked soul as he asks the eternal question "why?" He poses the question to Sappho, the ancient Greek poetess, whom he calls "sister" because, he says, they are alike in their poetic genius and in their abnormality:

Thee only of all; yet can no memory say
How many a night and day
My heart has been as thy heart, and my life
As thy life is, a sleepless hidden thing,
Full of the thirst and hunger of winter and spring,
That seeks its food not in such love or strife
As fill men's hearts with passionate hours and rest.
From no loved lips and on no loving breast
Have I sought ever for such gifts as bring
Comfort, to stay the secret soul with sleep.
The joys, the loves, the labours, whence men reap
Rathe fruit of hopes and fears,
I have made not mine; the best of all my days
Have been as those fair fruitless summer strays,
Those water-waifs that but the sea-wind steers,
Flakes of glad foam or flowers on footless ways
That take the wind in season and the sun,
And when the wind wills is their season done.[6]

She it was, he says, who first inspired him to sing the song of
their longings.

As brother and sister were we, child and bird,
Since thy first Lesbian word
Flamed on me, and I knew not whence I knew
This was the song that struck my whole soul through,
Pierced my keen spirit of sense with edge more keen,
Even when I knew not,—even ere sooth was seen,—
When thou wast but the tawny sweet winged thing
Whose cry was but of spring.[7]

He pleads with her to tell him what it is that the gods have given
him and her. She can supply the answer, he feels certain, because,
as a Lesbian, she is capable of more profound perceptions of love
and pain than he is. Then, from the night, the wind, and the sea
he fancies he hears her song, and his soul rises in lyric ecstasy.

Ah, then, what song is this, that here
One ear fulfilled and mad with music, one
Makes all the night one ear,
Heart kindling as the heart of heaven, to hear
A song more fiery than the awakening sun

[156]

> *Sings, when his song sets fire*
> *To the air and clouds that build the dead night's pyre?*
> O thou of divers-coloured mind, O thou
> Deathless, God's daughter subtle-souled—*lo, now,*
> *Now to the song above all songs, in flight*
> *Higher than the day-star's height,*
> *And sweet as sound the moving wings of night!*
> Thou of the divers-coloured seat—*behold,*
> *Her very song of old!*—
> O deathless, O God's daughter subtle-souled! [8]

Lafourcade calls "On the Cliffs" "the high-water mark" of Swinburne's poetry. Along with *Atalanta*, "The Triumph of Time," "Thalassius," and *Tristram of Lyonesse*, it may stand among the high peaks of his achievement. Nowhere in world literature is there a more inspired revelation of the innermost soul of the artist in his eternal struggle with the mysteries of life and self.

In long narrative poetry *Tristram of Lyonesse* is one of the supreme achievements of Swinburne's genius. Lafourcade says Swinburne began the poem in 1868, but lost his manuscript in a cab and had to start over.[9] In 1870, perhaps disgusted with Tennyson's publication of "The Grail," he worked on it again.[10] Lafourcade is also our authority for the statement that Watts-Dunton, before it was published in 1882, toned down some of the passages that he thought overly sensual.[11] His later version of the Tristram legend runs to about four thousand lines and one hundred and forty-four pages in the Bonchurch Edition. Divided into nine books, it is epic in character and style. The meter is iambic pentameter rhymed couplets, a device that is happily suited to the medieval story.

Nothing gives a more accurate indication of the growth of Swinburne's poetic genius than a comparison of this poem with the early version of the same story he had done at Oxford under the title *Queen Iseult*. The more masculine title is indicative of the much more masculine approach to the old love story in *Tristram of Lyonesse*. Gone are most of the algolagnia and the other suggestions of abnormality that mar *Queen Iseult*. The later Tristram does not yearn to be killed or tortured by Iseult, as had his earlier model. He prefers to love her in some of the most sensual scenes in English poetry. Nor is he so silly as to fall in love with her hair; he now loves the whole woman. Nor, after they arrive in

Cornwall, does Iseult have to carry him to her room. She sends her maid and companion Brangwain to sleep with King Mark (who, in the darkness, fancies his companion is Iseult) while she steals to Tristram's room and spends the night there.

Was this more masculine approach the result of Watts-Dunton's advice? Was it attributable to Swinburne's nature at this time making another effort toward normality—the same kind of response that had evidently led him to Mary Gordon in 1863? Or was there some other cause? We don't know. At any rate, the love theme in *Tristram of Lyonesse* is more authentically treated than in any other of Swinburne's poems. There are a few touches of algolagnia in that their love is mixed with some pain—their kisses, for instance, are described as "burning"—but, for the most part, this is a great and convincing story of the love of a man and a woman, told with sympathy and deep feeling.

The story is likewise handled with far greater skill than in the Oxford poem. *Tristram* begins on shipboard with Tristram and Iseult leaving Ireland for Cornwall. Iseult's mother's giving Brangwain the goblet with the love philter and instructing her to make sure that King Mark and Iseult drink it on their wedding night is skillfully worked into the narrative in a flashback, instead of being a major scene as it was in the early poem. And the business of Tristram's parentage and birth are handled in a few swift lines without stopping the chief movement of the story. Tristram's wanderings after leaving his angry uncle are omitted altogether. We end Book II with Tristram and Iseult making love in the forest in Cornwall, and we begin Book III with him in Brittany pining for her. When the scenes of sensual love between Tristram and Iseult become a bit tedious, Swinburne relieves them by injecting the hate motif with Iseult of the white hands— the wife Tristram abandons when he returns to Iseult of Cornwall.

The central theme of the poem is the intensity of the love between the chief protagonists. Here Swinburne rises to the heights in bursts of lyric fervor. After Iseult drinks the love potion, she is transformed from an innocent girl to a woman desperately in love:

> . . . *yea, she felt*
> *Through her own soul the sovereign morning melt,*
> *And all the sacred passion of the sun;*

[158]

> And as the young clouds flamed and were undone
> About him coming, touched and burnt away
> In rosy ruin and yellow spoil of day,
> The sweet veil of her body and corporal sense
> Felt the dawn also cleave it, and incense
> With light from inward and with effluent heat
> The kindling soul through fleshly hands and feet.[12]

After rescuing Iseult from the evil Palamede, Tristram takes her to a cave in the forest where their lovemaking rises to ecstasy:

> Here he caught up her lips with his, and made
> The wild prayer silent in her heart that prayed,
> And strained her to him till all her faint breath sank
> And her bright limbs palpitated and shrank
> And rose and fluctuated as flowers in rain
> That bends them and they tremble and rise again
> And heave and straighten and quiver all through with bliss
> And turn afresh their mouths up for a kiss,
> Amorous, athirst of that sweet influent love;
> So, hungering towards his hovering lips above,
> Her red-rose mouth yearned silent, and her eyes
> Closed, and flashed after, as through June's darkest skies
> The divine heartbeats of the deep live light
> Make open and shut the gates of the outer night.[13]

But there is more to *Tristram in Lyonesse* than sensuous verse. Swinburne tells his story and depicts his characters with a subtlety that reminds the reader of *Love's Cross-Currents*. Iseult of the white hands is, at the beginning of the poem, an innocent girl of sixteen. She is puzzled and hurt when Tristram does not consummate their marriage on their wedding night. But she grows into a fury when he leaves her for the Iseult in Cornwall. Vowing vengeance, she waits until he returns sick and wounded; then she administers the death stroke by lying to him that Iseult of Cornwall is not coming to him in answer to his dying request.

The charm of the story is heightened by Swinburne's philosophical comments upon, and interpretations of, the events. Quite in contrast to his earlier anger at God for permitting evil and injustice is his philosophical acceptance of fate when Tristram lies dying:

> . . . *Fate, that is fire to burn and sea to drown,*
> *Strength to build up and thunder to cast down;*
> *Fate, shield and screen for each man's lifelong head,*
> *And sword at last or dart that strikes it dead;*
> *Fate, higher than heaven and deeper than the grave,*
> *That saves and spares not, spares and dothe not save;*
> *Fate, that in gods' wise is not bought and sold*
> *For prayer or price of penitence or gold. . . .*[14]

The most serious flaw in *Tristram* lies in the fact that the love passion appears to be purely sensual. The lovers desire each other's physical being, nothing more. There is no tenderness, no deep sympathy, no delight in companionship—nothing of the spiritual grandeur that raises the love of man and woman to the sublime. Of course, Swinburne could have excused this fault on the ground that the love was caused by the philter, which inspired Tristram and Iseult with an insatiable physical longing for each other. But the events of the story imply that this was a love beyond the senses. It was more than sensual love that impelled a dying Tristram to ask Iseult to come to him; it was certainly more than sensual love that brought her over the sea to his deathbed.

Oddly enough, *Tristram of Lyonesse* is seldom anthologized. Yet it is a truly fine poem which throbs with life and drama. To omit it is to deny to a truly great poet, who all his life struggled against almost insuperable handicaps, the honor that is his due.

IV *The Burlesques*

Perhaps here is as good a place as any to discuss Swinburne's truly great sense of humor and his humorous writings. He seems to have considered such writings beneath the dignity of a great poet, for, with the exception of his parodies in verse, his most notable efforts in this direction he did not publish. Instead, he circulated them privately among his friends. Because of their intrinsic merit and because they present a side of Swinburne that the world knows little of, they should be published. It is hoped that they will be in the near future.

The verse parodies are delectable. They include tongue-in-cheek takeoffs on Tennyson ("The Higher Pantheism in a Nutshell" from the original "The Higher Pantheism"), Browning

("John Jones's Wife"—from the original "James Lee's Wife"), Elizabeth Browning ("The Poet and the Woodlouse" from her poem by the same title), Coventry Patmore ("The Person of the House" from his poem of that same title), Robert Lytton ("Last Words of a Seventh-Rate Poet" also from the original of the same title), Dante Rossetti ("Sonnet for a Picture" is from "Sonnets for a Picture"), and Swinburne himself ("Nephelidia"). In this last, Swinburne shows his good sportsmanship by wickedly parodying his weakness for adjectives and alliteration. All the parodies are so penetrating and so skillfully contrived that they constitute probably the greatest literary criticism Swinburne ever wrote.

Added to these should be such works as *La Fille du Policeman,* the fake reviews of Cossu and Clouet, *The Sister of the Queen,* perhaps the *Cannibal Catechism,* the dialogue in French in which Queen Victoria describes to her mother her seduction by Wordsworth, and numerous other quips from his letters. Essentially, of course, all these are in the spirit of that defiance of Victorian prudery and pomposity that had inspired his espousal of Pre-Raphaelitism and Baudelaireism and that underlay *Chastelard* and the *Poems and Ballads* of 1866. We can only regret that he had not always been able to temper his rebellion with the delicious humor that these works exhibit. His life would have been happier and his works would have benefited inestimably.

V *Swinburne's Contribution*

What is the true measure of Swinburne's achievement? What has been his effect upon English literature? Physically and psychologically handicapped by his personal shortcomings, he was unable to comprehend the whole of life or to treat of it convincingly. The happiness of true love, the expansion of identity that comes with marriage, the deeper understanding of the cycle of life that comes with having children and watching them mature—these were experiences that were never his. He was further restricted by the loss of his religious faith and by his consequent denial of mysticism. For all these reasons his verse never plumbed the profundities of life explored by Browning and Arnold, nor did he attain the lyrical heights of the verse of Keats or Tennyson. He must, therefore, take rank below all of them.

His chief services to English literature lay in two directions. He thrust aside the smug prudery of his times and dared to sing of the body and the senses as no one before him had done. He prepared the way for modern frankness in literature by making the love passion the subject of lyrical verse. As no one had before him, he turned into beautiful song the longings and frustrations of the sexually abnormal. His second contribution lay in his incomparable mastery of prosody. Even Tennyson acknowledged that he envied Swinburne's lyrical gift, and well he might. In his songs Swinburne taught the poets who followed him new lyrical possibilities of English verse. His resources for achieving rhythmical variety were apparently boundless. Perhaps nowhere are they better displayed than in his "The Triumph of Time," "Dolores," "Thalassius," and *Tristram of Lyonesse*.

Certainly Swinburne was one of the most learned of the English poets. Endowed with a remarkable memory, he ranged over the length and breadth of the history and literature of both ancient and modern times as few English poets ever did, but he carefully avoided Browning's obscurity and did not clutter up his works with abstruse references. What Swinburne had to say was sometimes said with verbosity, but it was always said artistically and clearly. With remarkable facility he could write a Latin satire or a French song or essay. His translations of the poems of Villon into English cause us to regret that he did not do more in this direction, for he had a real knack of catching the mood and flavor of the original in his translation.

Watts-Dunton's remark that Swinburne invented Walter Pater is, of course, an exaggeration, but it points up the fact that Pater learned much from Swinburne. So did Rossetti, Lord de Tabley, Ezra Pound, and many others, most of whom have not acknowledged their indebtedness. Even James Joyce, in his experimentation with the meaning that may be extracted from the sounds of words, was following Swinburne's lead. For if Swinburne proved nothing else, he aptly demonstrated that words have not only meanings but sounds which may be combined into music and rhythm to achieve a higher meaning than any lexicographer can express or than any mere message-hunting reader of poetry can ever comprehend.

Notes and References

Chapter One

1. Georges Lafourcade, *Swinburne: A Literary Biography* (London, 1932), p, 6.
2. Georges Lafourcade, *La Jeunesse de Swinburne* (London, 1928), I, 63-64.
3. Mrs. Disney Leith, *Algernon Charles Swinburne* (New York, 1916), pp. 8-9.
4. Cecil Y. Lang, ed., *The Swinburne Letters* (New Haven, 1959-1962), II, 82-83; hereafter referred to as *Letters*.
5. Irving Bieber, *et al.*, *Homosexuality: A Psychoanalytic Study* (New York, 1962), p. 117.
6. *Ibid.*, p. 41.
7. *Letters*, III, 10-11.
8. Edmund Gosse, *The Life of Algernon Charles Swinburne* (London, 1917), p. 26.
9. *Letters*, IV, 321.
10. Gosse, pp. 13-14.
11. *Ibid.*, p. 26.
12. Humphrey Hare, *Swinburne* (London, 1949), p. 15.
13. Photoduplicated from the manuscript in the British Museum by permission of William Heinemann Ltd.
14. Gosse, pp. 26-27.
15. *Letters*, VI, 6-7.
16. James Pope-Hennessy, *Monckton Milnes* (London, 1951), p. 146.
17. *Letters*, I, 256.
18. *Ibid.*, 78.
19. *Ibid.*, VI, 6.
20. Lafourcade, *Swinburne*, p. 47.

Chapter Two

1. A. C. Swinburne, *Two Unpublished Manuscripts* (San Francisco, 1927); these are in the Lilly Library at Indiana University.
2. *Letters*, III, 13, 14.

3. Oswald Doughty, *Dante Gabriel Rossetti* (New Haven, 1949), pp. 99-101.

4. *Ibid.*, p. 102.

5. John G. Millais, *The Life and Letters of Sir John Everett Millais* (London, 1899), I, 52, 55.

6. Helen Rossetti Angeli, *Dante Gabriel Rossetti* (London, 1949), pp. 217-24.

7. Charles Baudelaire, "Salon de 1859," *Curiosites Esthetiques,* ed. M. Jacques Crepet (Paris, 1923), p. 267.

8. Théophile Gautier, "Preface by the Author," *Mademoiselle de Maupin* (New York, 1944), p. xxvii.

9. *Letters*, II, 75.

10. Mrs. Georgiana Burne-Jones, *Memorials of Edward Burne-Jones* (London, 1906), p. 149.

11. *Letters,* I, 195.

12. *Ibid.,* V, 207.

Chapter Three

1. Lafourcade, *La Jeunesse*, II, 17-18. For most of Swinburne's unpublished works I am indebted to Professor Lafourcade's second volume of *La Jeunesse,* where extensive summaries are given with ample quotations.

2. *The Complete Works of Algernon Charles Swinburne,* Bonchurch Edition, eds. Sir Edmund Gosse and Thomas J. Wise (London, 1925), I, 118. Hereafter given as *Works.*

3. *Ibid.*

4. Lafourcade, *La Jeunesse,* II, 41. In the title the name is spelled "Iseult," but in the poem it is given as "Yseult."

5. *Ibid.*

6. Doughty, pp. 637-38.

7. Cecil Y. Lang, "Swinburne's Lost Love, *PMLA*, LXXIV (March, 1959), 123-30.

8. Lang, *Letters*, II, 342-43, dates this letter as 1874, but indicates uncertainty. Lafourcade, *La Jeunesse*, II, 128, dates it as 1873.

9. Lafourcade, *La Jeunesse,* II, 132.

10. *Ibid.,* 171.

11. *Ibid.,* 169.

12. *Ibid.,* 223.

13. *Ibid.,* 165.

Chapter Four

1. Lafourcade, *Swinburne,* p. 83.

2. *Ibid.,* p. 81.

3. Bieber, *et al.,* p. 28.

4. *Ibid.,* pp. 39-40.
5. Doughty, p. 323.
6. Ford Madox Hueffer, *Ancient Lights* (London, 1911), p. 26.
7. *Letters,* I, 46.
8. Bieber, *et al.,* p. 303.
9. Lafourcade, *Swinburne,* p. 191n.
10. Angeli, *Rossetti,* p. 77.
11. *Ibid.,* p. 216.
12. William Bell Scott, *Autobiographical Notes of the Life of William Bell Scott* (New York, 1892), I, 289-90.
13. *Letters,* VI, 92.
14. Lafourcade, *Swinburne,* p. 83.
15. *Ibid.,* p. 127.
16. Helen Rossetti Angeli, *Pre-Raphaelite Twilight* (London, 1954), p. 178.
17. *Letters,* VI, 245.
18. *Ibid.,* I, 51-53.
19. *Works,* XX, 436.
20. *Ibid.,* XIII, 419.
21. *Ibid.*
22. *Ibid.,* 423.
23. *Ibid.,* 426.
24. *Letters,* I, 88.
25. Pope-Hennessy, p. 134.
26. Marquis de Sade, *Selected Writings,* trans. Leonard de Saint-Yves (London, 1953), p. 10.
27. *Letters,* I, 53-54.
28. *Ibid.,* 66-67.
29. *Ibid.,* 75.
30. *Ibid.,* 78.
31. *Ibid.,* 44n., 223n.
32. Lafourcade, *Swinburne,* p. 129.
33. Hare, pp. 111-12.
34. Gosse, pp. 95-96.
35. Henry Adams, *The Education of Henry Adams* (Boston, 1918), p. 139.
36. *The Times,* (London) May 3, 1866, p. 14.
37. *Letters,* III, 278-79.
38. Lang, "Swinburne's Lost Love," 123-30.
39. *Letters,* I, 125.
40. *Ibid.,* 135.
41. *Ibid.,* 143.
42. *Ibid.,* 155n., 161n.
43. *Ibid.,* 183.

44. Gosse, p. 119.
45. William Meredith, ed., *Letters of George Meredith* (London, 1912), I, 55.

Chapter Five

1. *Works,* XIII, 159.
2. *Ibid.,* 163-64.
3. Lafourcade, *La Jeunesse,* II, 375-76.
4. *Ibid.*
5. Hare, p. 73.
6. *Spectator,* XXXV (June 7, 1862), 632-33.
7. *Letters,* I, 55, 58.
8. *Works,* VII, 351.
9. *Letters,* I, xxxii.
10. *Ibid.,* VI, 236-37.
11. *Works,* VII, 293.
12. *Ibid.,* 299.
13. *Ibid.,* 300.
14. *Ibid.,* 307.
15. *Letters,* I, 93.
16. *Works,* VII, 269.
17. *Ibid.,* 271.
18. Lafourcade, *Swinburne,* p. 130.
19. *Ibid.,* pp. 112-13.
20. *Letters,* I, 114.
21. *Works,* VIII, 38.
22. *Letters,* I, 136.
23. *Spectator,* XXXVIII (December 2, 1865), 1343-44.
24. *North American Review,* CII (April, 1866), 545.
25. Lord Houghton, "Mr. Swinburne's 'Chastelard,'" *Fortnightly Review,* IV (April 15, 1866), 543.
26. Charles Tennyson, *Alfred Tennyson* (New York, 1949), p. 359.
27. *Works,* XV, 122-23.
28. *Spectator,* XXXIX (March 31, 1866), 357.
29. *Letters,* I, 141n.
30. *Ibid.,* 140n.
31. *Ibid.,* 137-39.
32. *Ibid.,* 141.
33. Swinburne, *Poems and Ballads* (London, 1889), p. 197.
34. *Ibid.,* p. 305.
35. *Ibid.,* pp. 102-4.
36. *Ibid.,* pp. 133-34.
37. *Ibid.,* p. 217.
38. *Ibid.,* p. 46.

39. *Ibid.*, p. 50.
40. *Ibid.*, p. 51.
41. *Ibid.*, p. 54.
42. *Ibid.*, p. 7.
43. *Ibid.*, p. 73.
44. *Ibid.*, p. 96.
45. *Ibid.*, p. 100.
46. *Ibid.*, p. 174.
47. *Ibid.*, pp. 175, 176.
48. *Ibid.*, p. 230.
49. Lafourcade, *Swinburne,* p. 109; also *Works,* XVI, 365.
50. *Letters,* I, 99.
51. *Poems and Ballads,* p. 220.
52. Doughty, p. 281.
53. *Ibid.*, and Lafourcade, *Swinburne,* p. 106.
54. Lafourcade, *Swinburne,* p. 193.
55. *Works,* XVI, 132-33.
56. *Ibid,.* 137-38.
57. Hueffer, *Ancient Lights,* p. 148.
58. *Letters,* I, 156.
59. Lafourcade, *La Jeunesse,* II, 285.
60. *Works,* XVII, 67.
61. *The Novels of A. C. Swinburne,* ed. Edmund Wilson (New York, 1962), pp. 43-44.
62. *Ibid.*, p. 44.
63. *Works,* XVII, 251-52.
64. *Ibid.*, 180-81.
65. *Letters,* I, 224.
66. Swinburne, *Lesbia Brandon,* ed. Randolph Hughes (London, 1952), p. 30.

Chapter Six

1. *Letters,* I, 172.
2. *Ibid.*, 84-85.
3. *Ibid.*, 169-70. Swinburne's letter to Joseph Knight on August 3, 1866, shows that he had already read the *Athenaeum* review. I assume that the *Saturday* also came out on August 3, and that Lytton's letter arrived on that date.
4. *Ibid.*, 151.
5. J. W. R. Scott, *The Life and Death of a Newspaper* (London, 1952), pp. 14, 48, 49.
6. T. H. S. Escott, *Masters of English Journalism* (London, 1911), pp. 231-32.
7. *Ibid.*

8. Merle Mowbray, *The Saturday Review, 1855-1868* (New York, 1941), p. 221.

9. [John Morley] "Mr. Swinburne's New Poems," *The Saturday Review*, XXII (August 4, 1866), 145.

10. *Ibid.*

11. *Ibid.*

12. *Ibid.*

13. *Athenaeum* (August 4, 1866), 137-38.

14. *Ibid.*

15. *Ibid.*

16. *Letters*, I, 173.

17. *Ibid.*, 176-77.

18. William Michael Rossetti, *Swinburne's Poems and Ballads, A Criticism* (London, 1866), p. 36.

19. *Punch*, LI (November 10, 1866),189.

20. *The Examiner* (October 6,1866), p. 627.

21. [Carleton Green] "Mr. Swinburne and His Poetry," *The Light Blue* (January, 1867), pp. 10-15.

22. *Letters*, I, 195.

23. Lafourcade, *Swinburne*, p. 149.

24. *Works*, II, 67.

25. *Ibid.*, 72, 75.

26. *Ibid.*, 137.

27. *Ibid.*, 145.

28. *Ibid.*, 233.

29. *Ibid.*, 363.

Chapter Seven

1. *Works*, XVI, 372.

2. *Letters*, I, 146.

3. Harriet Jay, *Robert Buchanan* (London, 1903), p. 161.

4. *Letters*, I, 143.

5. *Spectator*, XXXIX (September 15, 1866), 1028.

6. *Works*, XVI, 371.

7. Robert Buchanan, "On My Own Tentatives," *David Gray and Other Essays* (London, 1868), p. 291.

8. *Works*, XVI, 430.

9. William M. Rossetti, *Swinburne's Poems and Ballads* (London, 1866), p. 7.

10. William M. Rossetti, *Dante Gabriel Rossetti: His Family Letters with a Memoir* (Boston, 1895), I, 295.

11. *Athenaeum* (November 3, 1866), pp. 564-65.

12. *Letters*, I, 212.

13. Swinburne, "Matthew Arnold's New Poems," *Fortnightly Review,* n. s. II (October 1, 1867), 428.

14. *Works,* XV, 90n.

15. *Letters,* VI, 264.

16. *Athenaeum* (January 29, 1870), pp. 154-56.

17. Sir William Hardman, *A Mid-Victorian-Pepys* (New York, 1923), pp. 78-79.

18. *Letters,* I, 192.

19. *Works,* XV, 212, 214, 215.

20. *Letters,* II, 101.

21. *Works,* XV, 29.

22. *Ibid.,* 7.

23. *Ibid.,* 13.

24. *Ibid.,* 39.

25. *North American Review,* CXI (October, 1870), 471-74.

26. *Ibid.,* 457-79.

27. *Ibid.,* 479.

28. *Ibid.,* 480.

29. Robert Buchanan, "The Fleshly School of Poetry: Mr. D. G. Rossetti," *Contemporary Review,* XVIII (October, 1871), 343.

30. *Ibid.,* 337, 338.

31. *Ibid.,* 343.

32. *Letters of Dante Gabriel Rossetti to William Allingham,* ed. George B. Hill (London, 1897), p. 292.

33. *Athenaeum* (December 16, 1871), p. 794.

34. *Ibid.,* 792-93.

35. *Ibid.,* p. 793.

36. Dante Gabriel Rossetti, *Poems* (London, 1870), p. 201.

37. *Athenaeum* (December 16, 1871), pp. 793-94.

38. Doughty, pp. 469-85 *passim.*

39. Robert Buchanan, *The Fleshly School of Poetry* (London, 1872), p. 3.

40. *Letters,* II, 137-38.

41. *Works,* XVI, 425.

42. Buchanan, "The Fleshly School of Poetry," 337.

43. Robert Buchanan, "The Monkey and the Microscope," *St. Paul's Magazine,* XI (August, 1872), 240.

44. *The Examiner* (November 20, 1875), p. 1304.

45. *The Examiner* (December 11, 1875), p. 1388.

46. *Ibid.*

47. *Athenaeum* (July 8, 1876), pp. 50-51.

Chapter Eight

1. *Letters,* II, 143n.
2. *Ibid.,* IV, 55-56.
3. *Works,* III, 171.
4. *Ibid.,* XIV, 3.
5. *Ibid.,* XVI, 12-14.
6. *Works,* III, 307.
7. *Ibid.,* 311.
8. *Ibid.,* 313.
9. Lafourcade, *Swinburne,* p. 195.
10. *Ibid.,* p. 202.
11. *Ibid.,* p. 292.
12. *Works,* IV, 46.
13. *Ibid.,* 70.
14. *Ibid.,* 151.

Selected Bibliography

PRIMARY SOURCES

The most complete collection of the works is the Bonchurch Edition of *The Complete Works of Algernon Charles Swinburne,* edited by Sir Edmund Gosse and Thomas J. Wise, 1925-1927, and published in London by William Heinemann Ltd. Because of Wise's reputation an accurate edition should be prepared. Several of the early works and some of the later works of an off-color character have been omitted from the Bonchurch Edition; its title is, therefore, misleading. When the complete works are reedited, all the strays should be included.

As things now stand, the best account of the early unpublished works, together with extensive quotations, is given in Georges Lafourcade, *La Jeunesse de Swinburne,* II, published in London in 1928 by William Heinemann Ltd. The first publication of the novel *Lesbia Brandon* is that edited by Randolph Hughes and published in London in 1952 by the Falcon Press. Hughes' voluminous commentary makes extravagant claims that have never been substantiated. An edition of the two novels *Love's Cross-Currents* and *Lesbia Brandon* was done in 1962 by Edmund Wilson and published in New York by Farrar, Straus & Cudahy.

The six-volume edition of *The Swinburne Letters,* edited by Cecil Y. Lang for the Yale University Press, was published from 1959 to 1962. It includes hundreds of letters never before published and is indispensable. In the preface to the first volume Professor Lang makes it clear that there are still many letters outstanding which may still appear. It is presumed that Mrs. Disney Leith's statement in the preface to her *Algernon Charles Swinburne* (New York: G. P. Putnam's Sons 1917), that she destroyed the family letters of Swinburne after the publication of her book, is correct.

BOOKS BY SWINBURNE

I. Collected Editions
Poems. 6 vols. London: Chatto and Windus, 1904.

Tragedies. 5 vols. London: Chatto and Windus, 1905.

Complete Works. 20 vols. Bonchurch Edition. London: William Heinemann Ltd., 1925-27.

II. Individual Works

The Queen Mother and Rosamond. London: Edward Moxon and Co., 1860.

Atalanta in Calydon. London: Edward Moxon and Co., 1865.

Chastelard. London: Edward Moxon and Co., 1865.

Poems and Ballads. London: John Camden Hotten, 1866.

Notes on Poems and Reviews. London: John Camden Hotten, 1866.

A Song of Italy. London: John Camden Hotten, 1867.

William Blake. London: John Camden Hotten, 1868.

Notes on the Royal Academy Exhibition. John Camden Hotten, 1868.

Songs before Sunrise. London: F. S. Ellis, 1871.

Under the Microscope. London: D. White [F. S. Ellis], 1872.

Bothwell. London: Chatto and Windus, 1874.

George Chapman. London: Chatto and Windus, 1875.

Essays and Studies. London: Chatto and Windus, 1875.

Songs of Two Nations. London: Chatto and Windus, 1875.

Note on the Muscovite Crusade. London: Chatto and Windus, 1876.

Erechtheus. London: Chatto and Windus, 1876.

A Year's Letters. Epistolary novel published in installments in *The Tatler*, August 25 to December 29, 1877, under pseudonym "H. Manners."

A Note on Charlotte Bronte. London: Chatto and Windus, 1877.

Poems and Ballads, Second Series. London: Chatto and Windus, 1878.

A Study of Shakespeare. London: Chatto and Windus, 1880.

Songs of the Springtides. London: Chatto and Windus, 1880.

Studies in Song. London: Chatto and Windus, 1880.

Tristram of Lyonesse and Other Poems. London: Chatto and Windus, 1882.

Mary Stuart. London: Chatto and Windus, 1882.

A Century of Roundels. London: Chatto and Windus, 1883.

A Midsummer Holiday and Other Poems. London: Chatto and Windus, 1884.

Marino Faliero. London: Chatto and Windus, 1885.

Miscellanies. London: Chatto and Windus, 1886.

A Study of Victor Hugo. London: Chatto and Windus, 1886.

Locrine. London: Chatto and Windus, 1887.

The Whippingham Papers. London: Chatto and Windus, 1888.

Poems and Ballads, Third Series. London: Chatto and Windus, 1889.

A Study of Ben Jonson. London: Chatto and Windus, 1889.

The Sisters. London: Chatto and Windus, 1892.

Selected Bibliography

Astrophel and Other Poems. London: Chatto and Windus, 1894.
Studies in Prose and Poetry. London: Chatto and Windus, 1894.
The Tale of Balen. London: Chatto and Windus, 1896.
Rosamond, Queen of the Lombards. London: Chatto and Windus, 1899.
A Channel Passage and Other Poems. London: Chatto and Windus, 1904.
Love's Cross-Currents. London: Chatto and Windus, 1905.
The Age of Shakespeare. London: Chatto and Windus, 1908.
The Duke of Gandia. London: Chatto and Windus, 1908.
Lesbia Brandon, ed. Randolph Hughes. London: The Falcon Press, 1952.

SECONDARY SOURCES

I. Bibliographical

Bateson, F. W. *The Cambridge Bibliography of English Literature*. Vol. III, 317-322. New York: The Macmillan Company, 1941.
Lafourcade, Georges. *La Jeunesse de Swinburne*. Vol. III, 583-600. London: Oxford University Press, 1928. Especially good for the early works, many of which have not yet been published. Must be used with caution because Lafourcade got much of his information from Thomas J. Wise, who is extremely unreliable. Must be checked against John Carter and Graham Pollard, *An Enquiry into the Nature of Certain Nineteenth Century Pamphlets* (New York: Scribner, 1934) to weed out the Wise forgeries.
Lang, Cecil Y. *The Swinburne Letters*. Vol. VI, 420-431. New Haven: Yale University Press, 1962. Though only a portion of the index, and with the information scattered throughout the six volumes of the letters, this is a good listing of the works.
Wise, Thomas J. *Bibliography of the Writings in Prose and Verse of Algernon Charles Swinburne*. Vol. XX of the Bonchurch Edition of *The Complete Works of Algernon Charles Swinburne*. London: William Heinemann Ltd., 1927. The most complete and detailed bibliography, but for reasons given above it must be used with caution and checked against Carter and Pollard's *Enquiry*.

II. Critical and Biographical

Adams, Henry. *The Education of Henry Adams*. Boston: Houghton Mifflin Co., 1918.
Allingham, William. *A Diary*. London: Macmillan and Co., Ltd., 1907. Personal recollections of Dante Gabriel Rossetti.
Angeli, Helen Rossetti. *Dante Gabriel Rossetti*. London: Hamish

Hamilton, 1949. The daughter of William Rossetti gives new information on both Dante Rossetti and Swinburne.

——. *Pre-Raphaelite Twilight*. London: The Richards Press, 1954. Though primarily a defense of Charles A. Howell and Dante Rossetti, this work adds still newer information on Dante Rossetti, Swinburne, and Howell. Because of the author's strong family bias, one must weigh carefully her unsubstantiated information.

Ashbee, Henry Spencer. *Index Librorum Prohibitorum*. London: [No publisher given], 1877. Not to be confused with the Catholic *Index*, this book gives private information on London publishers, especially John Camden Hotten.

Austin, Alfred. "Mr. Swinburne," *Temple Bar*, XXVI (July, 1869), 457-74. A strongly negative article on Swinburne which he answered in *Under the Microscope*.

Baudelaire, Charles. "Notes Nouvelles sur Edgar Poe," Introduction to Baudelaire's French edition of Poe's short stories in Vol. VI of *Nouvelles Histoires Extraordinaires*. Paris: Calmann-Lévy Éditeurs, 1857.

——. *Oeuvres Complètes*. Paris: Louis Conard, Libraire-Éditeur, 1923.

Beerbohm, Max. *Rossetti and his Circle*. London: William Heinemann Ltd., 1922.

Bevington, Merle M. *The Saturday Review*. New York: Columbia University Press, 1941. Explains the editorial policy that led to attack on *Poems and Ballads*.

Bieber, Irving, *et. al.* *Homosexuality: A Psychoanalytic Study*. New York: Basic Books, Inc., 1962. A psychoanalytic case study of abnormal sexuality.

Browning, Oscar. *Memories of Sixty Years*. London: John Lane, the Bodley Head, 1910. Gives personal recollections of life at Eton in Swinburne's time.

"Buchanan *versus* Taylor," *The Examiner* (July 8, 1876), 763. Gives a jocular account of the trial of 1876.

Burne-Jones, Mrs. Georgiana. *Memorials of Edward Burne-Jones*. London: Macmillan and Co., Ltd., 1906. Firsthand material on Swinburne's early days in London by the wife of one of his close friends.

Caine, Hall. *Recollections of Rossetti*. London: Cassell and Co. Ltd., 1928. Important anecdotes of Rossetti's last years.

Chew, Samuel C. *Swinburne*. Boston: Little, Brown, and Co., 1929. Excellent criticism.

Child, Ruth C. *The Aesthetic of Walter Pater*. New York: The Macmillan Company, 1940. Since Pater took many ideas from Swinburne and was closely associated with him, this affords a secondhand approach to Swinburne's aesthetic and philosophical principles.

De Sade, Marquis. *Selected Writings.* Trans. Leonard de Saint-Yves. London: Peter Owen Ltd., 1953.

Doughty, Oswald. *Dante Gabriel Rossetti.* New Haven: Yale University Press, 1949. Still the best, most comprehensive biography.

Friswell, James Hain. "Mr. Algernon C. Swinburne." *Modern Men of Letters Honestly Criticized.* London: Hodder and Stoughton, 1870. Contemporary criticism, mostly harsh.

Gautier, Théophile. *Charles Baudelaire.* London: Greening and Co., 1915. Good account by a contemporary.

————. *Mademoiselle de Maupin.* New York: The Heritage Press, 1944. Swinburne's first introduction to "art for art's sake" came through this novel.

Gilman, Margaret. *Baudelaire the Critic.* New York: Columbia University Press, 1943. An excellent critical biography and explanation of Baudelaire's critical and artistic philosophy.

Gosse, Sir Edmund. *The Life of Algernon Charles Swinburne.* London: The Macmillan Company, Ltd., 1917. The first full-length biography, it contains much source material. Somewhat biased and not always reliable because of Gosse's love of dramatization.

————. "Swinburne: an Essay," originally written in 1925 but first published in Vol. VI of Lang's edition of *The Swinburne Letters* (New Haven: Yale University Press, 1962), 233-48.

Hardman, Sir William. *A Mid-Victorian Pepys.* New York: George H. Doran Co., 1923. Personal anecdotes of Swinburne and others by a London publisher.

Hare, Humphrey. *Swinburne.* London: H. F. and G. Witherly Ltd., 1949. Interestingly written but not always reliable.

Hueffer, Ford Madox. *Memories and Impressions.* New York: Harper and Brothers, 1911. A breezy account of Rossetti, Swinburne, and the Pre-Raphaelites by a cousin of the Rossettis.

Hunt, W. Holman. *Pre-Raphaelitism and the Pre-Raphaelite Brotherhood.* 2 vols. London: Macmillan and Co., Ltd., 1905. An account of the early ideals of the movement by its founder.

Hyder, C. K. *Swinburne's Literary Career and Fame.* Duke University Press, 1933. Contains indispensable source materials.

Lafourcade, Georges. *La Jeunesse de Swinburne.* 2 vols. London: Oxford University Press, 1928. The best account of the years to 1866 in Vol. I and the most complete account as well as the best criticism of the early works in Vol. II.

————. *Swinburne.* London: Oxford University Press, 1932. The best biography, but it does not include recent and indispensable material.

Lang, Cecil Y. "Swinburne's Lost Love," *PMLA* (March, 1959), 123-

130. This most important essay presents a strong case to show that Swinburne's love affair was with his cousin Mary Gordon (Mrs. Disney Leith) rather than "Boo" Falkner.

Leith, Mrs. Disney. *Algernon Charles Swinburne*. New York: G. P. Putnam's Sons, 1917. Account by Swinburne's cousin who knew him as a child. Personal recollections.

Millais, John G. *The Life and Letters of Sir John Everett Millais*. 2 vols. London: Methuen and Co., 1899. An account of the early days of Pre-Raphaelitism.

Moore, George. *Confessions of a Young Man*. London: T. Werner Laurie, 1904. Personal recollections of Swinburne by a later member of the aesthetic movement.

Nicolson, Harold. *Swinburne (EML)*. London: The Macmillan Company, Ltd., 1926. A good critical study.

Pope-Hennessy, James. *Monckton Milnes*. London: Constable, 1951. Good recent biography of Lord Houghton; somewhat laudatory.

Rossetti, William M. *Dante Gabriel Rossetti: His Family Letters with a Memoir*. 2 vols. Boston: Roberts Brothers, 1895. Fiercely defensive of his brother; must be read with caution.

————. *Rossetti Papers, 1862-1870*. London: Sands and Co., 1903. Personal material but also to be read with caution.

————. *Swinburne's Poems and Ballads*. London: John Camden Hotten, 1866. A clever, strongly biased defense of Swinburne.

Satyricon of Petronius Arbiter. London: [No publisher given], 1899. This explains the insult in Buchanan's Gito reference to Swinburne in the *Athenaeum* review of *Poems and Ballads* on August 4, 1866.

Scott, William Bell. *Autobiographical Notes of the Life of William Bell Scott*. 2 vols. New York: Harper and Brothers, 1892. Candid and unbiased accounts of Swinburne and the Rossettis by personal friend; occasionally inaccurate.

Stedman, E. C. *Victorian Poets*. Boston: James R. Osgood and Co., 1876. Criticism biased in favor of Swinburne by one of his friends.

Tennyson, Charles. *Alfred Tennyson*. New York: The Macmillan Company, 1949. Gives new material on Tennyson's reaction to Swinburne.

Watts-Dunton, Clara. *Home Life of Swinburne*. London: A. M. Philpot, 1922. Account of home life at "The Pines" by Watts-Dunton's secretary, whom Watts-Dunton married.

Waugh, Evelyn. *Rossetti*. New York: Dodd, Mead and Co., 1928. An interpretive, witty biography written by a novelist.

Welby, T. Earle. *A Study of Swinburne*. New York: George H. Doran Company, 1926. Excellent criticism.

Wilde, Oscar. *Letters*. Ed. Rupert Hart-Davis. London: Harcourt, Brace & World, 1962. Shows closer association with Swinburne than Swinburne acknowledged.

Index

Index